the
GREEN BICYCLE
MYSTERY

by Antony M. Brown

Published by Mirror Books,
an imprint of Trinity Mirror plc,
1 Canada Square,
London E14 5AP, England

www.mirrorbooks.co.uk
twitter.com/themirrorbooks

ISBN 978-1-907324-69-7

First paperback edition

Printed and bound in Great Britain
by CPI Group (UK) Ltd, Croydon, CR0 4YY

Front cover illustration: Dave Thompson

COLD CASE JURY

presents...

THE GREEN BICYCLE MYSTERY

After finishing this book, readers are invited
to deliver their own verdicts and share their
theories on the Cold Case Jury website:
coldcasejury.com

ACKNOWLEDGEMENTS

I wish to thank all of the following for their help in writing and researching this book: Neil Bell, Simon Cole, June Cunningham, Iain Gately and David Hughes. This book would never have been written without the support of two people in particular: Paul Stickler, a partner in true crime, and Carla, my wife, who edited innumerable drafts and asked searching questions. At Mirror Books I would like to thank Julie Adams, Fergus McKenna, Paula Scott and Jo Sollis, also Ivor Game at the Mirrorpix archive for unearthing the original images they hold for this case.

CONTENTS

COLD CASE JURY

About Cold Case Jury: *Best Served Cold*

Preface: *Cowardice and Complicity*

PART ONE: *The Story*

PART TWO: *The Evidence*

ABOUT COLD CASE JURY

Best Served Cold

I agree with George Orwell, who famously lamented the decline of the English murder. He thought original murders were virtually extinct by the first half of the 20th Century, and that brutality had replaced ingenuity in pursuance of the ultimate crime. Gone were the days of assiduous poisonings, carefully laid traps and mysterious killings without apparent motive. These were now the preserve of thrillers, movies and, of course, dear Aunt Agatha. Fact had lost its frisson to fiction and reality was left somehow diminished.

There is a quality to a bygone murder that seems to set it apart from its modern counterparts. It was an era of etiquette and arsenic, of afternoon tea with a spoonful of malice. Modern Britain is too open, too honest even, to create the social conditions of the past that drove some to commit murder, often with an insidious craft that flummoxed the authorities of the day.

This last point is important. Like revenge, a venerable murder is best served cold. Unsolved. These are the intriguing cases that have several plausible solutions and have bequeathed us enough evidence to let us debate what probably happened. These are the masterpieces of murder, to quote the title of an Edmund Pearson book, the dark art that would be hung upon the cold walls of a Tate Criminal Gallery. These are the cases for the Cold Case Jury.

Does this mean that these crimes were perpetrated by the Machiavellis of murder? No, an unsolved crime from Orwell's golden age of murder does not imply its criminals were more deviously clever than today's. Undoubtedly some were, but the truth is that many of these cold cases would be solved by today's higher standards of professionalism and scientific methods of detection. Even the assassination of President Kennedy in 1963, arguably the most analysed murder of the last century, spawned a vast conspiracy-theory industry largely because of a flawed autopsy. Whether this was by malign influence or honourable incompetence is a quicksand best avoided here. My point is that, had the autopsy retrieved the bullet fragments from the President's brain, subsequent forensic analysis would have revealed the type of gun that terminated a presidency that bright November day and the shadows of doubt, as well as an industry, might have disappeared.

So, am I re-investigating these cold cases, unearthing fresh evidence or presenting new theories to shed new light on old crimes? Sometimes, yes, but my overriding goal is to present the reader with an interesting case for which the verdict is open to doubt. My task is to take the reader back in time to witness the events leading up to a violent or suspicious death; reconstruct how it occurred according to the different theories; and present evidence to the reader as in a real court. I hope to bring these crimes back to life, showing how the drama might have unfolded, emphasising the timeless interplay of the people involved and presenting the historical stage on which they acted. In reconstructing a cold case theory I prefer to use narrative's present tense – dialogue. Some of it is verbatim, drawn from trial or inquest testimony. The rest is more a work of imagination, yet always governed by the facts and theories of the case, connecting the evidential dots by plausible lines of narrative.

I hope I am also an impartial advocate – the Cold Case Advocate, if you like. My aim is to show the strengths and weaknesses of each theory and then you have your say. I'm hoping you will give your verdict at the Cold Case Jury website **(coldcasejury.com)**. Where over time an overall verdict from the Jury will emerge for each case.

My final task is to present my views on the case. But my view is only one.

The verdict always lies with you, the jury.

PREFACE

Cowardice and Complicity

"It has long been an axiom of mine," announced Sherlock Holmes in *A Case of Identity*, "that the little things are infinitely the most important." After reading this compelling real-life case, I suspect members of the Cold Case Jury will agree. It concerns the shooting of a young cyclist in rural Leicestershire months after the end of World War I. Your verdict will hang on the interpretation of key details: a squashed bullet found at the scene; a stranger calling a woman by her name; a dead crow discovered near the body. Are these 'little things' merely coincidences, or are they central to solving the case?

Our story is also a study in cowardice and complicity. Fearing he would become the prime suspect, an important witness fails to come forward to help the police. He remains silent until his involvement is eventually uncovered. Does this pattern of concealment point merely to moral cowardice or to someone who has a guilty secret? All of these issues – and more – will be for you to decide.

The Green Bicycle Case is nearly a century old. In this book new evidence is placed before the Cold Case Jury, enabling the complete story to be told for the first time.

The result is in your hands.

Antony M. Brown, *February 2017*

PART ONE

The Story

This is the true story of the death of Bella Wright in Leicestershire in 1919. To this day the case remains a topic of conversation in those parts and beyond.

With domineering hand she moves the turning wheel,
Like currents in a treacherous bay swept to and fro.

From *The Consolation of Philosophy* by Boethius.

Chapter 1

A LAND FIT FOR HEROES

In a lonely lane running through rural Leicestershire, a solitary bicycle lies on its side, its metal frame catching the glow of the fading evening light. Its back wheel slowly turns about its axle, producing a soft clicking; a rhythmic sound, soothing like the ticking of a study clock.

Next to the bicycle, lying at an angle across the road, is a young woman. She is partly on her back, partly on her left side, with her right hand almost touching the mudguard of the rear wheel. Her legs rest on the roadside verge, where fronds of cow parsley and rosebay rise above luxuriant summer foliage. On her head sits a wide-brimmed straw hat, daintily finished with a ribbon and bow. She is dressed in a pastel blouse and long skirt underneath a light raincoat, the pockets of which contain an empty purse and a box of matches.

The blood-flecked coat tells a story: the afternoon had threatened rain, but the evening has brought death. The left side of her head is heavily bloodstained, and her brown eyes are fixed in a cold, lifeless stare. From underneath her hat, creeping fingers of crimson slowly percolate through the weathered gravel. A macabre trail of bloodied bird tracks leads back and forth from the body to a nearby wooden gate, its top sporting the same marks like a sinister satanic rite. From the gate, a path has been beaten across the wispy grass of a small meadow, snaking towards a golden field of corn beyond. It appears to have been made by human feet – and recently.

The turning wheel comes to rest with a final click. On the other side of a high hedge, a grazing rabbit in the meadow freezes, its ears pricking up. For a fleeting moment there seems to be no sound or movement anywhere, not even a summer breeze to tremble the full-bodied trees that line the lane. Nature holds her breath, as if even she has been shocked into silence by the senseless death.

A deep bellow, like the tolling of a bell, echoes across the fields. Further along the lane, amid a sea of flicking tails and lolloping heads, a farmer nonchalantly herds his heifers. In a few languid minutes, accompanied by a raucous cawing of quarrelling crows in distant tree tops, the grisly scene will be discovered.

And the mystery will begin.

The singular circumstances of a dead cyclist lying in an isolated country lane with bloodied bird tracks to and from the body could have been lifted from a Sherlock Holmes story. Indeed, it is easy to imagine the perplexed farmer in the sitting room of 221B Baker Street explaining his shocking discovery to a pensive Holmes puffing on his calabash pipe. If we blur the lines between fact and fiction for a moment, the dates fit. The unfortunate cyclist died in the summer of 1919, when the world's most famous detective was alive, at least to the readers of *The Strand Magazine*, with more cases yet to be solved.

There was no hawk-faced detective for Leicestershire Constabulary to call upon to solve this intriguing case, although its officers acquitted themselves admirably, as you will see later. After a lucky break, and through dogged detective work, a suspect was tracked down and stood trial for murder. However, the jury returned a 'not guilty' verdict and the case went cold – the ideal temperature to fascinate criminologists, which it has done for nearly a century. The nature of the crime, the period in which it is set, the character of the victim and the sinister behaviour of the suspect each contribute to make this a classic case to put before the Cold Case Jury.

I am inviting every reader to take a seat in the jury box. I will take you back to the crime scene to reconstruct several versions of how events unfolded, according to the theories that have been advanced to explain the young cyclist's untimely death. At the end of this book you will find my view of the case, but it is your opinion that matters. As in a real court of law, the verdict always rests with you, the jury.

How did the cyclist die? This is the question on which you are invited to reach a verdict. In this case there are three available verdicts: murder, manslaughter and misadventure. You are being asked to look at the evidence, decide what is plausible and then deliver your verdict online.

Chapter 1

As well as examining the three major theories, in a later chapter you will be presented with recently unearthed evidence. Kept in a police safe for decades, it is a document that might change the whole complexion of the case and is being published in full for the first time. Like all the other evidence, it will be introduced and analysed at the appropriate time, but it will be for you to decide how it affects your eventual verdict.

For now, you need to be introduced to the victim and understand the time in which she lived – and died. For the circumstances surrounding this unexplained death owe as much to the prevailing character of the period as to the idiosyncrasies of those involved.

The young woman lying dead in the isolated lane next to her bicycle was 21-year-old Annie Bella Wright, known as Bella, a Leicester factory worker. She had been a Jubilee baby, born in the year that Queen Victoria celebrated 60 years on the throne, and three years before the 19th Century was consigned to history. Born near Melton Mowbray in rural Leicestershire, she was the eldest of seven children born to farm labourer Kenus and his wife, Mary Ann.

Bella was seven years old when she began attending the school at Somerby, a small village five miles south of Melton Mowbray. An old school photograph shows the taciturn-looking teacher with her pupils. It is a typical Edwardian school scene. At the front, girls are dressed in dark blouses and white, dress-length pinafores with dark boots and socks. At the back, leaning against a brick wall, is a line of mischievous-looking young lads wearing white-collared shirts, hands stuffed in trouser pockets.

Two years later the family, forever following the vagaries of a farm labourer's employment, moved a few miles further south to Knossington, where Bella finished her six years of schooling. This was an age when eldest daughters in large, poor families drew a difficult lot. A short education was usually followed by long hours of domestic service until, with a little luck, a good husband came along. Bella Wright was no different. She started school late, having assisted her mother with the housework from a young age, and left her studies early to start work. Her father, illiterate and uneducated except in the ways of farm life, wanted his eldest to make her own way in the world, and provide much-needed financial support back home for the growing family.

In the summer of 1910, shortly after Edward VII's funeral at Westminster Abbey attracted a vast gathering of Europe's nobility, Bella turned 13, and her schooldays ended. She entered the service of a gentleman living a few miles south of her home, and was employed there for several years. By the time Bella left to seek new opportunities, the Singer strike in Scotland had made national headlines, and underlined the difficulties women faced in the workplace.

The sewing machine manufacturer employed 12,000 workers in Clydebank, of which a quarter were women. In March 1911, the management reassigned three repair workers from a team of 15 women. The repair workers were paid a fixed wage but the remaining dozen women were paid piece-work, strictly according to the amount they produced. The management insisted that the remaining women undertake unpaid repair work in addition to their existing duties, resulting in a significant pay cut if the women worked the same number of hours as before. Within two days over 10,000 workers had walked out in protest. The three-week strike ended when the company threatened the non-unionised workforce.

Yet the pressure for social change was growing inexorably. In June 1913, while Bella was working as a parlour maid in the household of a wealthy Leicestershire family, suffragette Emily Davison walked onto the racetrack during the Derby. She was hit by the king's horse and fatally injured. Whether she planned to commit suicide is a question for debate, but her death shocked the sensibilities of polite society. Yet, ironically, it would be the death of one man that would shake the foundations of the old order, and eventually advance the feminist cause like no other. In June 1914, two weeks before Bella turned 17, Archduke Franz Ferdinand was assassinated in Sarajevo. The domineering hand of an assassin had turned irrevocably the wheel of fate. Five weeks later, on the eve of war, the Foreign Secretary gravely told the House of Commons that "the lamps are going out across Europe". Four years later, when the lamps were re-lit, they cast a different light.

During the First World War, over a million women had streamed into factories, taking up the more lucrative roles originally held by men who had been drafted into the Army. Many worked in dangerous munitions factories, where exposure to hazardous substances turned the skin yellow, which led to the women being nicknamed 'canaries'. The patronising label glossed over their suffering and sacrifice.

Ill-health was not the only risk, and some shared the

same fate as many men on the frontline. In July 1918, part of a munitions factory at Chilwell, near Nottingham, was destroyed in a massive blast that was heard 20 miles away. Eight tons of TNT, equivalent to almost a thousand artillery shells, had somehow ignited. The tragedy left over 130 women dead. Less than three dozen bodies were recovered, identified and buried. The remains of the rest were interred in a mass grave, today marked by a simple blue plaque in a local churchyard; a modest tomb for the unknown worker. But there was little time for remembrance. Production resumed the following day, and returned to normal levels within a month.

Tens of thousands of women worked in other factories, less dangerous but equally important to the war effort, making uniforms, boots and equipment needed by the troops. The face of labour was changing. It had a feminine look.

Bella was part of this silent revolution. In May 1917, after seven years in domestic service and a short spell as a shop assistant, she embarked on a new career as a factory worker in Leicester. Her first position was a shoe machinist, followed by work in a glove and hosiery factory. Even with the burden of the war, there was still demand for life's luxuries, especially from the well-heeled. While employed there, Bella heard the news of the Armistice, which brought joy to a war-weary people. Schools, factories and shops closed early as jubilant, flag-waving celebrations swept the country.

At the Western Front events were more subdued, the visceral emotion one of relief. The gunfire and shelling had ended, giving way to an awful silence. Many men could not rejoice, the memories of fallen comrades uppermost in their minds. Others were engulfed in an anxious helplessness: what were they to do now? They knew all too well that they would have to pick up the pieces of their former lives. But, to a man, the desire was the same: to come home.

The British Army had to demobilise hundreds of thousands of troops. It was a tediously slow process. During the ensuing winter months, bored men tried to pass away the time by exercising, playing football and cards. Whoever was given a 'white ticket' had priority to come home, and these were given to 'key men' deemed to have important skills in vital industries. It transpired that key men were often those who had joined the hostilities later, for precisely the same reason. Effectively, it became a last-in-first-out policy, and provoked controversy and widespread rancour. In addition, abuse of the system was rife. The well connected often received tickets, while men who had fought for the entire campaign were left waiting, and moaning bitterly.

And even though hostilities had ended, troops continued to be lost. The Front remained a dangerous minefield of tree stumps, mud holes, abandoned equipment and live ammunition. As the countryside was cleared, accidents involving live shells only added to the enormous casualty list of the war. Worse was to come. By early 1919, Spanish flu struck with devastating force at home and abroad. Men who had survived the war succumbed to this most virulent form of influenza, one that disproportionately killed the young. In less than 36 hours, one regiment in France recorded over 150 cases – and 30 deaths. Some troops already infected with the virus travelled home to their families, and then fell ill. In circumstances that are just too distressing to contemplate, some mothers watched sons die within days of their homecoming.

Most troops returned home during 1919, but not to "a land fit for heroes" that was promised by Prime Minister David Lloyd George. It was just the opposite. Mass demobilisation led to mass unemployment and social tension. Many men returned to find that their previous jobs had been taken by women, normally working for less, or the role had been made redundant by mechanisation. Strikes were rife, with over two million workers involved in industrial action during the calendar year. Striking dock workers held up supplies of fuel and food. As a consequence, large numbers of dominion soldiers experienced poor conditions and delays in repatriation. This had further consequences. At a camp in North Wales, Canadian troops were on half-rations with no coal for heating in freezing and overcrowded huts. In March the troops mutinied. Five soldiers were killed and nearly two dozen injured when the riots were suppressed.

With a fearful eye on the Bolshevik revolution in Russia, the government was deeply concerned that the industrial strife would lead to revolution, particularly in some of the more populous industrial towns. To make matters worse, large numbers of firearms had been brought back illicitly by demobilised troops. Some simply did not want to part with their weapon, while others would not relinquish prized trophies captured from the enemy. The number of revolvers and rifles in private ownership grew.

It was against this backdrop of social and economic upheaval that, in early 1919, Bella Wright changed jobs, becoming a factory hand at Bates Rubber Works, a pneumatic tyre manufacturer based at St Mary's Mills in Leicester. Pneumatic tyres had been popular ever since John Dunlop developed them in 1888 to dampen the jarring to his son's tricycle from riding over coarse streets and rough ground. Thirty years later, St Mary's Mills had a booming business. Shift working ensured that production was extended throughout the day and into the night to keep up with the demand from bicycle and car manufacturers. The demand from the latter was increasing each year. In 1904 there were slightly fewer than 10,000 motor cars in private ownership in Britain. By the start of the war, this figure had mushroomed 15 times over. A few years after the war there would be over two million vehicles on British roads, half in private ownership.

Motor cars were the preserve of the wealthy, and would remain so for decades to come. For the rural working class, personal transport was by bicycle. A revolution in cycling had occurred 20 years previously. Until the 1890s 'high wheeler' bicycles with ludicrously large front wheels were perceived as a machine for adventurous pursuit. The invention of the 'safety bicycle', featuring equally sized wheels, a steerable front wheel, and a chain drive to the rear wheel (a design we would recognise as a bicycle today), transformed cycling into an everyday activity. Crucially, cycling became accessible to women, who for the first time had a method of personal transportation. Little wonder that feminists viewed the humble bicycle as a 'freedom machine', and huge numbers of middle-class women took up cycling.

As bicycles became safer and cheaper, more women

enjoyed not only the recreation cycling provided but the unprecedented mobility that ushered in a greater independence from the home. It also transformed female fashion. Voluminous and restrictive dresses, corsets and ankle-length skirts, impractical for cycling, were quickly discarded. By the outbreak of the war, cycling was a popular means of transportation for both men and women. For girls like Bella, who worked in the cities but lived rurally, away from the crowded suburbs, it was an essential method of travel.

Unlike domestic service, factory work was hot, noisy and dusty, but it had its compensations. Even though Bella worked the late shift, starting at 2pm and finishing at 10pm, she was able to socialise with girls of her own age. She had two close friends. Sisters Sally and Gertrude Ward were co-workers at St Mary's Mills, and especially close because their 18-year-old brother, Archie, a Navy stoker, was involved with Bella. It was an unofficial engagement, but everyone understood they were a couple and expected them to marry after he had been demobilised. Why there was no official engagement is not clear. Perhaps Bella had some doubts, or he had.

Bella was not gregarious, and would often keep her own counsel, but she was sociable and affable, and appears to have enjoyed her social life, including occasional day trips and 'shops outings' with co-workers. When her shift ended, she would cycle the three miles back to Stoughton (pronounced stoh-ton), where her family now lived in a small cottage annexed to the village school. Her father was a cowman for a local farmer, her brother Philip a wagoner on the same farm.

Chapter 1

Bella was in her prime, attractive rather than beautiful. She had a full face with a clear complexion, gentle brown eyes and dark hair. She certainly drew glances from young men. Her mother stated that during the last year of her life an army officer on a motorcycle had been admiring Bella and paying her compliments. Mother and daughter found intimate conversation difficult, leaving us to conjecture about the identity of the officer or whether his attentions were welcomed or not. It has implications for what follows.

Bella Wright worked at St Mary's Mills for only five months before the wheel of fate turned on a lonely Leicestershire lane. I have sketched some of the social conditions that were prevalent while she worked there – it was a time of troop demobilisation, changing aspirations of women, growing unemployment, rising social and political tensions, and cycling for personal transport as well as recreation. All these threads are entwined and woven into the backcloth of our story. It is now time to tell the events of the Green Bicycle Mystery.

Chapter 2

THE TURNING WHEEL

In the pages that follow, I will take you back to the sleepy villages and quiet lanes of rural Leicestershire to reconstruct the events that led to the untimely death of Bella Wright. Later, you will see how the drama might have unfolded according to each of the three theories that have been advanced to explain what happened. All the re-enactments are based on trial testimony, police statements and various secondary sources.

Our story begins on the day of the tragedy, Saturday, 5 July 1919. The place is the small black-and-white timbered cottage attached to the school at Stoughton, where Bella lives with her family.

2:30pm. Bella was roused by loud, chinking shrieks from outside the small cottage. She recognised the alarm instantly. It was a blackbird, which often gave panicked cries when a kestrel or carrion crow strayed too close to its nest. She yawned, rubbed the sleep dust from the corner of her eyes,

Chapter 2

and glanced at the face of the clock on the chest of drawers by her bed in the cramped room. She rose, washed her face in the bowl on top of the drawers, and peered up through the mullioned window. The sky was mostly grey, with some blue patches that gave hope of a summer's day. The canopies of nearby birch and elm swayed in the breeze. Sighing, she selected a pastel blue blouse, something summery at least, with a long skirt.

She took the few steps from the bedroom to the front room, which served as the kitchen as well as the living room. Her mother was washing clothes in the corner copper.

"Glad to see you're up at last," her mother commented.

"I need my lie-ins after a long week of late shifts," replied Bella.

Mary Wright squeezed out the water from a white shirt. "The factory is no place for a woman, if you ask me. Just you mind to be up bright and early for church tomorrow."

"Yes, I will, mother," Bella replied. Her mother made the same comments every Saturday.

"There's some water in the kettle," her mother continued, nodding in the direction of the range, "and there's some loaf left on the table." Bella made herself a cup of tea and a slice of buttered toast.

"What are you doing today?" Asked her mother, wringing out the water from another shirt.

"I'm really behind with my letters. My friends must be wondering what's become of me. And I must write to Archie, too."

"Make sure you do it today, then. And you can post one

of mine when you go." Her mother nodded again in the direction of the range. Above it was a mantelpiece, and sticking out behind a carriage clock was an addressed envelope. Bella nodded. There could be no further procrastination – once her mother asked for something, she expected it to be done promptly.

She finished her toast before collecting some writing paper and her fountain pen. Sipping her tea at the kitchen table, she began to write. After the usual pleasantries to one of her friends, she began to complain about the weather. Showers had been common – it did not feel like summer at all.

The last letter she wrote was to her boyfriend, Archie Ward. She was so looking forward to seeing him again, she wrote. After the usual small talk and warm musings, she finished the letter with an affectionate sign-off. She addressed the envelope to *HMS Diadem*, Archie's ship, which was permanently moored at Portsmouth. After sealing it, she closed her eyes and brought the back of the envelope to her lips. This vicarious kiss would be her last. In the aftermath of the tragic events that were to follow, Archie was given compassionate leave and the letter forwarded to the Ward family home. Like a love letter sent through time, it was to arrive days after her death and delivered only heartbreak.

6:10pm. After tea, Bella scooped up the letters, including her mother's behind the mantelpiece clock. She found her mother taking in the washing from the line in the small garden.

"Is it going to rain?" queried Bella.

Chapter 2

"They'll dry faster by the range. You going out?"

"I'm going to Evington to post my letters. And I've got yours." Bella patted the letters sticking out of her jacket pocket.

"You can find a penny on the mantelpiece for the stamp."

"Isn't it one and ha'pence now?"

"Oh, I keep forgetting."

"I've got sixpence, anyway. Pay me back later." Bella turned and took hold of her bicycle, which was resting against the whitewashed back wall, and pushed it towards the gate.

"Are you going to see Margaret later?" her mother inquired. Bella looked blankly. "Your cousin! She's at Uncle George's with her family."

"Oh yes, of course! I haven't seen her in ages, and I can't wait to see little Marjorie and baby James." She had never seen her cousins once-removed.

Mary Wright unpegged a white blouse from the washing line and placed it into the basket at her feet. Bella pushed open the wrought-iron gate and walked the few steps into the adjacent lane. Sweeping the long skirt under her, she mounted the saddle and started her leisurely cycle to Evington, a nearby village to the north west of Stoughton. Mother and daughter would never speak to each other again. It had not been a moment of loving embraces and farewells – sudden death steals such comforts.

For a city dweller, the journey from Stoughton would be far from quiet. Skylarks serenaded as they rose from the fields, while corn buntings sang loudly from their perches, as if in competition. At one point on the journey, a volery of excitable long-tailed tits seemed to follow Bella, flitting between trees, tails bobbing, chirping incessantly. Yet, to a country girl, these sounds were commonplace. This was tranquillity.

Bella reached the junction with Shady Lane, where sycamores lined the narrow road like a natural cathedral, tall trunks rising like columns to support a vaulted canopy of green. In the summer it was common to see bicycles of sweethearts propped by the tree trunks. Bella particularly enjoyed cycling through here on a hot, cloudless day when the intense sunshine was broken by the canopy, giving instant relief, and producing mazy, dappled patterns on the road surface. On a day like today, however, Shady Lane was dark, cool and lonely. The warm and wet conditions had spurred verdant growth everywhere. Bella had never seen the hedgerows and verges so thick with tall nettles, cow parsley and hawthorn.

As Bella approached Evington, she met another cyclist travelling towards her. It was Mrs Powers, who worked at the post office. In fact, the post office was part of a general store and joinery business run by a Mr Rowe. The shop was a converted front room, with a proper storefront and a well-dressed window. To the left was a pair of black garage doors, above which was a sign saying 'ROWE Carpenter Joiner'. It was something of a one-stop shop. Here you could buy confectionery, ices and teas, post letters and order a coffin, all at the same time. Sadly, in a few days, Rowe would build Bella's simple coffin.

"Hello, Mrs Powers," Bella said, as she applied the brakes and gently came to a halt. She stepped off her bicycle.

Kathleen Powers did the same. "Hello, Bella."

"I was just on my way to the store."

"I'm on my rounds – a few letters to deliver. What did you want?"

"I have some letters to post."

"Oh, I can take them back with me, if you like."

"I need some stamps too."

"That's all right, dear. I will stamp them – you can pay me later."

"No, I have the money." Bella took out her purse and handed over a two-shilling piece along with the letters from her jacket pocket. Mrs Powers glimpsed the address on the uppermost envelope as she placed them into her satchel.

"How's Archie?" she asked, handing back three sixpences and some coppers in change.

"Oh, he's fine, I think." Bella laughed coyly. "He's still down in Portsmouth. I hope he gets demobbed soon, but they say it could be months."

"It will come round soon enough, just you wait and see. These will be in the post as soon as I get back." She paused, looking skywards. "I think it may be getting brighter."

Above, Bella saw streaks of blue among a few brooding dark clouds. "I might be a little overdressed in this oilskin, don't you think? It's hard to cycle in."

"Well, you never know when it might rain, with this weather we're having at the moment. Anyhow, I'd better finish my round."

"I'd better head back too." Bella turned her bicycle around and pushed off. She swung by the cottage and swapped her oilskin for a light raincoat, and spoke briefly to her 17-year-old brother, Philip. He was not interested in cycling with her, he said. She called out for her mother, but there was no reply. Noticing the time on the mantelpiece clock, she decided to leave immediately to give herself plenty of time at her uncle's and still be able to return home before nightfall.

7:25pm. At a red-brick house in Gaulby, a village seven miles east of Leicester, there was a knock at the door. "That's 'em groceries," George Measures said to his son-in-law, who jumped up from his chair. Measures waved him down. "I'll get it, Jim," he said. He swung his peg leg from the foot stool and grabbed his walking stick from the floor by his armchair. With his bushy beard, Measures looked like a Long John Silver who had been cast away on a remote island. He hobbled to the door.

"Bella!"

"Hello, Uncle George."

"What a surprise," he said. "Have you come to see your cousin?"

"I have."

"Come in, girl. It's been some time since you came last. You were with that young lad… I forget his name."

"Archie," she replied, stepping over the threshold.

"That's right, Archie." Never one to shy away from giving an opinion, he added: "A straight young man, if I'm a good judge of character. You could do worse, lass."

Bella ignored the comment. Measures closed the door and followed Bella into the living room. "This is Jim, Margaret's husband," he said, gesturing to James Evans, a well-built young man standing by the fireplace with a toddler clinging to his leg.

After exchanging pleasantries, Bella crouched by the toddler. "You must be Marjorie." The youngster turned her face away. "How old is she now?"

"Eighteen months," Jim replied.

"And this is baby James," George said, picking up a bundle of swaddling from a crib.

"Oh, you are gorgeous," Bella cooed, taking the baby gently from her uncle.

"Margaret is having a nap," Jim explained. "She'll be down soon."

There was another knock. "That's 'em groceries now!" Measures said, hobbling back to the front door.

Bella felt a little awkward being left so soon in the presence of only Jim, whom she had never seen before. "Shall we see who that is?" Bella said to the baby. She followed her uncle, who had opened the door to Charles Palmer and his wife, Elizabeth, carriers from Illston On The Hill, a nearby village.

"This is my niece," Measures said. "She lives at Stoughton."

"I thought so," Elizabeth Palmer replied. "Doesn't she look like her mother, Charlie?" He husband grunted in the affirmative.

There was a little small talk about the weather before Bella took her cousin-once-removed back into the living room.

As Measures settled up with the Palmers he spotted an unshaven man wearing a grey flat cap sitting casually on a green bicycle outside his cottage.

"Is that fella with you?"

The Palmers looked over the hedge behind them. "No," said Elizabeth.

"What the devil's he doin' there," Measures said, taking an instant dislike to the stranger.

"He was cycling with your niece not five minutes ago."

Measures was surprised. "He arrived with Bella?"

"Yes, they passed us when we were by the church, didn't they, Charlie?" Her husband nodded.

"Are you sure it were 'im?"

She craned her neck to take another look at the man. "Oh yes, it's definitely him. I was sitting in the van and I saw them go by together. Is anything wrong?" Measures shook his head, but stared coldly at the stranger. He did not like the idea of an unshaven man accompanying his niece, who was already spoken for. Or, at least, he thought she was spoken for. At 61 years old he had strong views on such matters, having been raised with Victorian moral values. He bid the Palmers good night, and took the groceries into the kitchen.

Returning to the living room, Measures fell into his armchair, lifted his peg leg onto his stool, and puffed pensively on his pipe, wondering why a stranger appeared to be lingering outside his cottage.

"So, are you working, Bella?" Jim enquired.

"Yes, at the tyre factory. I'm on the late shift, but it's more fun than being in service. I've made some good friends." Bella turned her attention to the baby in her lap and waited for her cousin.

7:45pm. Looking dishevelled and tired, Margaret came downstairs. Bella immediately recognised her, having last seen her when she was a 14-year-old girl. She was weightier and more buxom.

"Bella!" Margaret said. "It has been too long."

"Yes, it has. When mother said you were visiting, I had to come."

The conversation between the cousins flowed freely for half an hour, during which time Measures remained silent, his thoughts preoccupied by the stranger. He supposed that the man would have left by now but he wanted to make sure. He hobbled to the front door.

"There's a man waitin' outside," Measures informed his niece when he returned to the living room. His tone was accusatory. "Is he with you?"

"What man? There's no man waiting for me, Uncle."

"Well, there's a man out there who looks old enough to be your father. He needs a damn good shave, too," Measures said in disgust. "It looks like he's waitin' for you. He's walkin' up an' down. Why's he doin' that?"

Jim walked to the front window and peered out. "Yeah, there's a man out there with a bicycle."

Bella looked a little uncomfortable. "I wonder whether it is the man who overtook me on the road. He said he had come from Great Glen. I don't know why he would be outside."

"You spoke to him?" Measures asked indignantly.

"It was just polite conversation, Uncle."

"You should know better, girl. You don't want to be invitin' trouble with strangers."

"Well, perhaps I should stay for a bit longer and he will go."

Her uncle was now like a terrier with a bone. "You must know something about him."

"I don't know him, Uncle. He's a perfect stranger. He met me on the road and rode with me, that's all."

"He's probably taking a breather, father," Margaret interjected. "There's nothing to trouble you."

But Measures was troubled. He had observed that Bella appeared to be unflustered by the presence of a man lingering outside; she had not even moved from the sofa to take a look. "Strangers don't hang around," he growled. "They go their own way."

"Well, perhaps he's lost," Margaret suggested, trying to placate the waspish manner of her father.

"He ain't askin' where to go."

"If he's still there when I leave, I'll give him the slip," Bella reassured her uncle. "I can easily get ahead of him."

Measures looked at his niece sceptically and was about to add something else when Jim intervened. "I'll take a look a little later, George. I'm sure he won't be there much longer." Measures grunted as he stuck his pipe back into his mouth, and fell mute again. The conversation between the cousins resumed.

8:35pm. "No sign of him now," Jim announced, after returning from a brief reconnoitre outside.

"I'd better be on my way," Bella said, sounding relieved.

"Before you go, let's have a look at your bicycle," Jim said. "You mentioned you had a problem with it?"

"Yes, I think there's something wrong with the rear wheel," Bella said, rising from her chair. "I had to stop on the way over to take a look."

Chapter 2

Everyone congregated outside the front door, Margaret cradling the baby, Measures holding Marjorie, and Bella holding a spanner her uncle had fetched. Jim was kneeling beside the bicycle, which was standing by the cottage gate. His attention was soon drawn to the freewheel (the rear-sprocket mechanism). A few moments later he had diagnosed the problem. "There's far too much give. You see?" Bella nodded, peering at the rear wheel hub as Jim moved part of the mechanism.

"It's getting cold, isn't it?" Margaret remarked to her cousin. "Just as well you brought your coat!"

"Hello, Bella!" Agnes, the younger daughter of George Measures, opened the gate and walked towards the gathering. Jim quietly took the spanner from Bella as the three cousins talked. After a few minutes, he looked up.

"I think that should do it, but you need to ride home carefully."

"I will," Bella replied, taking hold of the bicycle. Jim held open the gate while she took the few steps into the lane, her relatives following. Almost immediately, and seemingly out of nowhere, the unshaven man on the green bicycle freewheeled from the direction of the church, before dismounting and pushing it the final few yards. He stopped adjacent to Bella and said in a distinctively squeaky voice, "You have been a long time. I thought you had gone the other way."

There was an uncomfortable silence, during which Margaret noticed her cousin blushing. Jim stepped into the breach. "That's an unusual colour for a BSA," he remarked, pointing to the man's bicycle.

"Pea green," replied the unshaven man, dismounting. He spoke as if his voice had been mangled, its deep undertones squeezed to let out a high-pitch squeal. There was a distinctive accent too, which Jim thought was cockney. It certainly was not local. "It's a deluxe."

"I've got a BSA, too. May I take a look?"

"Be my guest. It's a heavy machine."

Jim took hold of the bicycle and knelt beside it. Agnes noticed the stranger muttering something to Bella, who laughed discreetly. "I see you have three-speed gears," Jim observed, pointing to the control box on the right handlebar.

The stranger approached him. "Yes, I've just had its control cable repaired."

Margaret gently pulled Bella aside. "Are you sure you don't know him?" she whispered.

"No, he's a stranger," Bella reiterated softly. "He overtook me on the road, that's all." Her cousin was not convinced – she had witnessed Bella's reaction when the man had first spoken to her. There was a familiarity between them, she was sure of it. Her instincts also told her this man was not suitable for her cousin to associate with, but she held back from saying so. She did not want to worry Bella, although it was the apparent lack of anxiety shown by her cousin that added to her suspicions.

"This back-pedalling brake is most unusual," Jim commented.

"Yes, it works from the crank to the rim."

"I've never seen anything like it before."

"Well, I've had the bike several years now."

George Measures studied the stranger intently. He was

small, about five feet six inches. It was difficult to guess precisely because the stranger was wearing a grey cap, which made him look a little taller. He had short brown hair flecked with grey. His dark eyes, too close together for the old man's liking, were capped by large eyebrows. He had a broad face with a soft, attenuated jaw and a thin upper lip. The corners of his mouth turned downwards, giving him a naturally surly look. He had a sallow complexion, with a moustache of stubble under a large, pointed nose and a dark shadow of growth on his chin. He wore a shabby grey suit, shirt and tie, trousers tied with bicycle clips near the ankles, and black boots. He was carrying a raincoat over his shoulder.

8:45pm. "Well, I'd better be going," Bella announced. She approached her uncle, who still clutched his granddaughter in his arms. "Bye-bye, Marjorie," she said, kissing the toddler on the check.

"Make haste, girl, and hurry home," Measures said solemnly.

Jim and Margaret wished Bella goodbye and a safe journey home, although the farewell was muted given the awkward presence of the stranger. Bella started to push her machine up the gentle incline toward the church. The man turned his green bicycle around and walked beside her, the two chatting sporadically.

"I don't like the cut of his jib," moaned Measures, as he watched them depart. "Did you catch his name?" Jim shook his head.

"I didn't speak to him," his daughter replied. Turning to her husband she remarked discreetly, "Bella must have known that man, don't you think?"

"Yes, of course she does."

At the top of the hill, the cyclists mounted their bicycles and disappeared from view. It was the last time Bella was seen alive by any of her relatives.

9:20pm. "C'mon now!" Joseph Cowell smacked the rump of a recalcitrant cow with his birch stick. It bellowed and walked through a wooden gate into the road where it joined the small herd. The cattle walked ponderously along the Via Devana, an old Roman road that ran between Leicester and Market Harborough. It was a thoroughfare that passed just to the south of a small village, Stretton Parva (today called Little Stretton). The lane was flanked by high hedgerows and tall trees, occasionally punctuated by a field gate leading to pasture or meadows.

Cowell was bringing the cattle to a field nearer his home at Elms Farm. Behind them, black angry clouds darkened the sky. To the west lighter clouds had parted, allowing the setting sun to paint the countryside in sepia tones. In only a few minutes it would sink below the horizon and the eerie long shadows would vanish into the gathering gloom.

Not long before the turning to Stretton Parva, Cowell saw something on the roadside a hundred yards distant. He thought it was a horse rug that had rolled off the back of a passing trap, but as he drew nearer he realised it was a person lying across the road. "Whoa!" he called out, holding his stick horizontal to halt the cattle. He walked forwards.

"Stone the crows," he muttered to himself. He could see that a young woman had fallen from her bicycle. She was quite still. As he knelt, he saw the woman's bloodied face and a pool of blood extending from underneath her hat. The girl was lying diagonally, partly in the road, partly on the grass verge in front of a wooden field gate. Blood slowly trickled from both nostrils. Seeing she was not conscious, he scooped her up in his arms. Her body felt limp; her head rolled backwards. He moved her out of the road onto the grass, where he bent over her, placing two fingers first on the side of her neck and then under her nose. She felt warm, but there was no pulse and no breath. "Ye God, have mercy!" he exclaimed, staggering backwards onto the road.

After he had recovered from the initial shock, Cowell picked up the bicycle from the road and leaned it against the wooden gate. He then ushered his cattle forward, the clopping hooves trampling over the blood stains on the gravelled road. When his beasts were safely deposited in a field some yards further down the lane, Cowell turned and ran back to the farm for his horse and cart. He then rode to the nearest police station to summon help.

10:30pm. When Police Constable Alfred Hall arrived at the scene, natural light had virtually slipped away into darkness and the temperature had fallen noticeably. In the road three men stood next to a horse-drawn milk cart. The yellow light of a lantern hanging from the back of the cart illuminated the body of a young woman lying on the grass verge.

PC Alfred Hall was stationed at Great Glen, a larger village to the south of the Via Devana. Aged 31, he had been in the force for nine years, although for 18 months he had been stationed with the Royal Garrison Artillery in France after he enlisted in June 1917. He was an imposing man, tall and handsome, with penetrating eyes and a bushy handlebar moustache. He was proud to the point of being stubborn, but his pride was matched by his tenacity and sense of duty.

One of the men peeled away and greeted Hall. "I've left a message with Dr Williams at Billesdon," Cowell said. "He'll be 'ere soon."

"Who are these men?"

"Naylor and Deacon." The two young men nodded an acknowledgement but said nothing. "I sent 'em when I got my float from the farm. They stayed while I came for you. Make sure nobody interfered."

"Has the body been moved?" Hall asked, approaching the lifeless form in the grass.

"Aye, I thought she 'ad come a cropper, so I took 'er off the road. She looked knocked out at first."

Hall knelt by the body, Cowell peering over him. The constable observed that the body was still warm, the limbs flexible. He took out his electric torch and shone it on her face. The left side was bloodied, especially around the nose and mouth. Her left eyeball was bulging, as if swollen, the right eye half closed. He flicked the beam of light to the plaited straw hat, which appeared to be congealed with blood. "The hat," he said, observing that it was still on the girl's head, "did you place it there?"

"It were on her head when I found her." Hall surmised that it was probably pinned. He shone his torch onto the body. There was little blood on her clothes, which were not torn or dishevelled. Hall carefully examined the pockets of her raincoat, discovering an empty purse and a box of

Flag matches in her left pocket. He inferred she might have been left-handed, although this was of little consequence.

"Do you know who she is?" Hall asked.

Cowell shrugged his shoulders. "Not from Stretton, that's for sure."

"Where exactly did you find the body?"

Cowell walked a few steps to the side of the road. "The head was pointin' to middle o'road," he said, gesturing to a pool of blood by the roadside, "and her legs were on the grass. The body was slanted."

"And the bicycle?"

"Lyin' next to her. Its wheels were on the road, but the seat and bars were touching the grass."

"Which way was the front wheel pointing?"

"That way."

Hall looked in the direction indicated by Cowell. "Towards Leicester?"

"Aye, and the back wheel was near the shoulder."

"So, her feet were pointing this way but," Hall said, turning half circle, "her head was pointing this way, towards Gaulby?"

"You got it."

It appeared the young woman had fallen off her saddle. "Where's the bicycle now?"

Cowell raised his lantern, illuminating the gate against which the bicycle had been propped. "I moved it off the road." Both men walked the few steps to the gate and, with Cowell providing the light, Hall knelt down and made a cursory inspection. He noticed a few drops of blood on one pedal, but nothing else of significance. There was certainly nothing to suggest foul play.

Hall stood up. "Looks like she's fallen and hit her head badly."

Cowell shook his head. "Aye, tragic."

"Can we get the body off the ground before the doctor arrives?"

Cowell instructed his men to retrieve a wooden sheep hurdle from a nearby field and position it by the body. The four of them lifted the young woman onto the make-shift stretcher, which was then placed in the back of the milk float.

10:40pm. The men shielded their eyes from the headlamps of an approaching car, which slowed and stopped by the cart. Dr Edward Williams opened the door and stepped out. The headlights remained on, piercing the gloom like two searchlights.

"She's 'ere, Doctor."

"I can see that, thank you Cowell." He approached the cart and, clambering on board, saw the lifeless body of a young woman lying prostrate among a scattering of empty urns. He touched her skin. The body was still warm, and he surmised she had not been dead two hours. He noticed blood under her nose and in her mouth. After a few minutes examination, he declared, "Sudden haemorrhage, I think."

PC Hall turned to Cowell. "Where can we move the body?"

The farmer thought for a moment. "The ol' chapel, I suppose," he replied, pointing in the direction of Stretton.

"Doctor, let's get the body inside so you can examine it properly." Hall turned to Cowell. "Take the body to the

Chapter 2

chapel and get some candles. We'll meet you there."

"Will do," replied the farmer, climbing into the seat of the cart. He instructed one of his men to walk ahead with the lantern.

Picking up the reins, Cowell urged the large shire forwards. The constable watched respectfully as the horse and cart turned at the junction by the fingerpost. Only a year before he had seen the bodies of the dead and dying carried from the muddy fields of northern France in a similar way. He could not help the memories intruding; it was a mental reflex, as involuntary as any physical one. As the sound of clopping hooves and jangling urns faded into the calm of the night, Hall inspected the scene with the doctor, shining his torch on the blood stains by the roadside.

11pm. The disused chapel at Stretton Parva was a small, rectangular red-brick building with a pitched roof. Looking more like a mundane outhouse than a place of worship, the only clue to its former role was a stone plaque engraved with the words "Free Chapel" embedded in a gable wall. It was a suitable place to keep the young woman's body overnight.

As Dr Williams approached, he saw the gentle glow of candlelight issuing from its two sash windows. PC Hall was wheeling in the girl's bicycle through the entrance to the right. He followed, closing the door behind him. In the centre of the room the men assembled around a table illuminated by four flickering candles. On it was sprawled the fully clothed body of the young woman.

Cowell repeated to the doctor how he discovered the body. Hall informed him that he had inspected briefly both the body and the bicycle and had found nothing suspicious. Williams moved the woman's head from side to side, feeling her skull and face, as if he was giving a macabre massage. "Extensive blood on the hair and the left side of her face," Dr Williams announced, stating the obvious. "There's also bruising on the left cheek just below the eye." He motioned for a candle to be brought nearer to take a closer look. "Yes, it's quite a vivid bruise, too."

"It seems to have an indentation in the skin," Hall commented.

"I can see that, Constable. She would sustain that by falling."

The cursory examination soon concluded. "I don't think we can do any more for the poor girl," Williams said.

"What's the cause of death, Doctor?"

"Oh, I would say sudden haemorrhage and collapse, Constable."

"Can I report that to my superintendent?"

"You certainly can. I really must be getting back," he said, placing his hat on his head. "Goodnight, all."

Alfred Hall nodded as the doctor walked to the door. One by one, he bid the others goodnight until he was left alone. He straightened the body on the table and placed her arms on her chest. He wanted the young woman to have dignity in death. He had not forgotten the carnage of war, when fine young men were often reduced to cuts of meat scattered across the filthy mires of the battlefield. Many soldiers had experienced the horror of picking up a pair of boots only to find that each contained a foot, or finding a stray helmet still strapped to a head. Bodies that had been hurriedly buried in no man's land were often disinterred by repeated shelling, sometimes forcing a limp, waxen arm to rise out of the mud. Like a ghoulish goodbye from an unknown warrior, the hand would stir in the wind or from a blast shockwave until the rats picked the flesh clean. In the war death had been dehumanised and, with it, life itself had been immeasurably devalued. He would make sure this body was treated with respect.

Hall blew out the last candle and secured the chapel door behind him. His thoughts were dominated by the girl on the table. Even though he had no knowledge of medicine, he found it hard to believe that a young woman would simply drop dead from exhaustion or a haemorrhage in the middle of a cycle ride. More plausibly, she could have fallen from the bicycle and died from head injuries, but there would be evidence of some kind to point to this conclusion: skid marks on the road or markings on a tyre where it had hit an exposed flint, perhaps. He knew from his war experiences that a haemorrhage issuing from the nose and mouth typically bloodies all the face and clothing at the front of the body. Yet, in this instance, it had only affected one side of the face and there was almost no blood on the woman's clothes or bicycle.

As he mounted his bicycle for the ride home, the only thing of which the constable was certain was that he needed to thoroughly re-examine everything in the cold light of day.

COLD LIGHT OF DAY

Members of the Cold Case Jury, Mary Ann Wright experienced one of the worst possible nights for a parent. Although Bella was 21 years old, she was usually home promptly, and always informed her mother of her plans. Her mother knew something was wrong, but there was nothing she could do but wait. And worry. There was no way to communicate at that late hour. Unless there was a clear sky with a full moon, nights in rural areas were pitch black, making cycle rides along pot-holed roads hazardous. This was a time of few telephones, when personal communications travelled at the speed of train or steamer. Even reports in the local newspaper were often days old. To a younger reader, life a hundred years ago, without a smartphone, access to the internet or mass media, would have felt like solitary confinement.

By daybreak on Sunday, anxiety was paralysing Mary Ann's thoughts. In the morning she went to the post office at Evington to report her eldest child as missing. The details were telegrammed to the police, but PC Alfred Hall would not hear of the report until later. He had risen early to revisit the scene of Bella's death. The following reconstruction is largely based on PC Hall's police report, written five days later.

We pick up the story on the morning of Sunday 6 July 1919.

6am. Absorbed in his thoughts, PC Hall cycled along the Via Devana. The road surface and the vegetation beside it were covered in a wet film. There had been the faintest sprinkling of rain during the night. There was dampness on the ground and in the air, but nothing more. Hall was greatly relieved. Rain would have erased the evidence he hoped to find.

He slowed as he approached the field gate where he had been summoned less than 10 hours before. He carefully cycled around the blood stain that was clearly visible on the road. He flicked the kickstand with his foot, and left his bicycle standing in the middle of the road. It would serve as a sign for cyclists and horse-drawn traffic to slow down. He looked down the road, towards Gaulby, and noticed it inclined steadily. It was not a steep gradient, by any measure, but it extended over several hundred yards at least. Anyone cycling down the hill towards the dip in the road, opposite the field gate where the young woman was found, would have been able to gather momentum quite easily. Was this a factor in the case? Hall noted it as one of the questions he wanted to answer.

As PC Hall surveyed the scene, he imagined Sherlock

Holmes telling him, "You know my methods, Constable. Apply them." He visualised the detective clambering over the road like a crab, carefully examining every stone and mark, and this is precisely what Hall did. The dampness had not removed the large bloodstain a yard from the roadside, although there was a small stream of blood running from it, parallel to the grass verge. In his mind's eye, he saw the young woman lying there as Cowell had described. For two hours he searched the sides of the road, the hedges and dykes, but he found nothing of significance. He could see no skid marks on the road to suggest that the young woman had fallen accidentally while cycling.

There was something puzzling him, however. If the bicycle was found in the position that Cowell had reported, where there was a stream of blood by the roadside, there should have been more blood on it. He revisited the chapel to examine the bicycle again, but there were only a few spots on one pedal, as he had observed the night before. With more questions than answers, he headed home for lunch.

3pm. Still troubled, Hall returned again to the scene and found bird tracks by the foot of the rickety wooden gate, which was tied to the fence post with frayed rope. There was a procession of bird footprints from gate to road and back again, six in either direction. He inspected the gate more closely, finding plenty of markings and splashes of dried mud on the worn rails and braces, and on the top there were two more claw marks – this time smeared in blood. Clearly, a bird had perched on the gate with bloodied feet. Hall thought it odd that a bird would be hopping around a human body so soon after death, while it was still warm. Hall retraced his steps to the road. He inspected the bloodstains once more before mounting his bicycle. He slowly rode the short distance home for tea.

6pm. After a hectic day, PC Alfred Hall made his way to the Via Devana for a third time and in possession of a new fact. From a recent missing persons report, the police had tentatively assigned a name to the deceased: Bella Wright. He again searched the same stretch of the Via Devana for something that would make sense of how Bella had died. Over an hour later, his Holmes-like patience and eye for detail was rewarded. About six yards from the large bloodstain he found a spent bullet in the middle of the road. It was depressed into the surface, lying in a hoofmark, and appeared to be deformed, as if trodden upon. Hall inferred that it had been kicked from where the head of the victim had lain, possibly by passing cattle or farm vehicles. The area had not been cordoned off because it was not perceived as a crime scene. Hall prised the bullet from the road and examined it closely. Drawing on his army experience, he was sure it was a .455 calibre bullet fired from a pistol or revolver. He felt certain it had killed the young cyclist – it strained credulity to believe that it was merely a coincidence that a bullet was lying so close to a dead body.

7:30pm. Hall revisited the scene with Joseph Cowell, who once again showed the constable the exact position where he had found the body less than 24 hours before. After inspecting the road, the two walked to the field gate. "This is where I placed the bicycle after I removed it from the road," Cowell said. The two men looked into the meadow of shin-high grass, bordered on all sides by high hedgerows and trees. "That looks like a track to me," Cowell pointed out casually.

"By Jove, it is," Hall replied, unhooking the rope tie. He pushed open the gate and followed an improvised path that had been cut through the grass, weaving into the distance. It had been made quite recently. The constable followed it to the corner of the meadow, where it petered out. Some yards away there was a stile leading into a field of chest-high corn. He tried to find a path or footprints in the cornfield, but all he found was a dead crow lying near to the stile. The path only heightened Hall's suspicions. "This was no accident," he told the farmer. "I'm sure of it. I'd better get Dr Williams again."

7:55pm. Hall cycled through Gaulby, quite unaware of the village's significance to the case, and headed north east. Not long after leaving the village, he ran into Dr Williams, who was walking along the lane from his home in Billesdon.

"Evening, Constable," Williams said cheerily.

Hall stopped, but remained seated on his bicycle. "Doctor, it's about the young woman who you examined last night."

"Oh?"

"I've picked up a bullet near to where her body was found."

"And you think it might be related to the poor girl's death?"

"Yes. I think she was shot."

"At Stretton? Surely not!"

"Well, I'm certain she did not die accidently. You need to examine the body again. Will you come back with me?"

Williams held up his medical bag. "House call, old chap,

but I have an appointment over at Great Glen at eleven tomorrow morning. How about I call in at Stretton on my way?"

"Tomorrow morning's no use to me, Doctor."

"Well, I think it will keep…"

Hall interjected firmly: "If you won't come, I shall get someone else."

"I will finish my visit and then go back to Billesdon for my car. I should be with you in less than an hour. Will that do?"

"Yes, thank you." Hall turned around his bicycle to leave.

"To save time, why don't you go straight back, get some water and wash the blood away from her face?"

"Good idea!" Hall pushed off and sped down the lane, his tyres humming on the road.

8:15pm. Carrying a bowl of water and a cloth, Hall unlocked the door to the chapel and entered, removing his peaked hat. The girl's body was lying neatly on the table as he had left it, but daylight now revealed the heavy bloodstains, dried and brown, on her straw hat, forehead and the left side of her face. He noted there was none on her raincoat.

The passing of the hours had also made death more evident. He tried straightening Bella's head but there was resistance. Whereas the previous night the body had been warm and supple, as if the young woman had been merely unconscious, now it was cold and stiff with rigor mortis. He might as well have been touching the table. Life has warmth and colour; death is cold and grey.

Like many of his generation, Hall had experienced the coldness of death during the war. The sight of a man opened up like a gutted fish from his shoulder to his waist by shrapnel, or soldiers swallowed alive by the glutinous filth of deep craters, had been commonplace. Those who were seriously injured and unable to move in the shell holes scattered across no man's land were the most unfortunate. With enemy fire and shelling making it too dangerous for a rescue attempt, the dying became entombed in the mud-filled mires along with rotting corpses, horse cadavers, burnt-out vehicles and discarded equipment. Unable to fend off even insects, they would be covered in a fur of bluebottles, while cockroaches crawled over their exposed wounds and rats chewed on their raw flesh. The pitiful groaning was unceasing, like the continual roar of waves on a beach, and could be heard even during shelling. In pain, in despair, and enduring the darkest hours of existence, the cries of these young men were always the same: they called out for mum. All those haunted by hearing those calls had one simple request. "Should I die," they would say to their comrades, "tell my mother that I died instantly."

Hall looked at the still body on the table. The skin of the right cheek had a waxy, yellow appearance with a tint of a bluish-grey, the same cold hue as her lips. The left cheek was covered in dried blood. He dampened the cloth and began to gently wash the dried blood from Bella's face. Even in death, he thought, cleansing the face was an intimate and tender act, like a mother washing a child. Slowly moving the cloth down her cheek, he lifted the veil of blood that had partially covered Bella's face since her death. And there, below her left eye, was a bullet wound.

He wrung out the bloody cloth in the bowl and waited for the doctor.

Chapter 3

8:40pm. Dr Williams stood next to PC Hall beside the makeshift mortuary table. "At least we have some daylight," he said. "It was such poor light last night, wasn't it?" To Hall, it sounded as if the doctor was already making excuses for his superficial examination the night before. It was regrettable that a Licentiate of the Royal College of Physicians had ignored the circumstantial evidence that pointed away from a brain haemorrhage: the lack of blood on the victim's clothing and bicycle. Hall resisted the urge to mimic Sherlock Holmes in *The Adventure of Silver Blaze* by asking rhetorically: "What about the curious blood splatter on the raincoat?" To which the doctor would have denied there was any, setting up the wonderful retort: "Indeed, that is the curious thing." Instead, Hall pointed deferentially to the puncture wound on the left cheek. "What do you think?"

"Oh, yes," replied the doctor in surprise, as if it had been the first time he had seen the body. "That looks like a gunshot wound, Constable." He bent over to examine Bella's face more closely. "Do we know who the poor thing is?"

"We have a name," Hall replied cautiously, "but it's not been confirmed."

"Ah, I see," the doctor said. "Is she local?"

"I cannot say any more, I'm afraid."

"Quite so."

Williams noted that the left cheek had been scratched and the left eyelid and eyeball were also injured, probably as a result of the fall to the ground. He then focused his attention on the obvious wound. "There is a puncture wound about one inch beyond the lateral canthus and about half an inch below." For Hall's benefit, he traced the two dimensions with his index finger from the corner of the eye. "You see, the puncture is surrounded by a collar of chafed skin, classic signs of a gunshot wound."

From his jacket pocket he removed a leaded pencil which he inserted into the aperture. The pencil went upwards and backwards into the brain. "A projectile has clearly penetrated the zygomatic bone. This appears to be the entrance wound. We will know by tracing its trajectory through the body." He unpinned Bella's blood-stained straw hat and passed it to Hall.

"It looks like it has gone through the hat too," the constable observed. The doctor looked up and saw that Hall had pushed his index finger through a small hole on the top right of the crown of the hat. Williams parted her hair, which was thickly matted with congealed blood. At the back of her head, about three inches above the right ear, was an oval wound approximately one-and-a-half- inches long and half-an-inch wide.

"That looks like an exit wound," Hall remarked.

"Indeed it does, Constable. This young woman has been shot, for sure. There needs to be an autopsy."

Members of the Cold Case Jury, without the tenacity and vigilance of Alfred Hall one can only wonder what might have happened in this case. This was a more deferential age when people were less likely to question the opinion of authority, including doctors. It is great credit to Hall that he not only asked questions but literally got on his bike to find the answers.

The next morning, Mary Ann Wright had the unpleasant task of formally identifying the body of her daughter. Dr Williams, assisted by Dr Phillips, then performed the autopsy. It confirmed what was already known from the second examination. There was a bruise over the left check, about an inch in diameter, in the centre of which was a small puncture wound. There was a larger exit wound over the second and upper third of the right parietal bone, at the back of her head. The brain had been severely lacerated. The doctor was puzzled by dark marks around the entry wound and excised a piece of skin from the left cheek and preserved it in a jar of formalin for further examination. The post-mortem discovered that Bella was not a virgin, but there were no signs of sexual assault or activity at the time of death {see *Exhibit 3 for the full autopsy findings*}.

On the Monday morning, Superintendent Herbert Taylor visited the scene, paying particular attention to the curious blood stains on the gate. A search was conducted of nearby fields and Taylor picked up the dead crow from the cornfield. He discovered its feet were covered in congealed blood, and matched them to the bird tracks on the gate. He then removed the crow for further examination. In my reconstruction, bird tracks were also found near the gate, a detail which was not included in PC Hall's report but taken from Russell Wakefield's *The Green Bicycle Case* (1930). In researching his book, Wakefield had spoken to Taylor, who is almost certainly the source of this detail.

By Monday afternoon, the police knew that Bella Wright had died from a gunshot wound, yet the local evening papers did not convey this information. Under the headline

'Woman Cyclist's Death', The *Leicester Mercury* reported that a nameless young woman was believed to have had a seizure and fallen from her bicycle near Stretton Parva, where she had been found dead. It was uncertain whether the death was a direct result of the seizure or the fall, the story said.

At the same time the police were printing handbills that stated that Annie Bella Wright was found with a bullet wound through the head. The small posters, which were a common method of requesting further information, were widely circulated throughout the area and to all police forces across the country the next day. A £5 reward was offered for information.

The police had already interviewed George Measures, his daughter and her husband. Consequently, the handbills provided detailed descriptions of both the unshaven man and his green bicycle. The police requested that, if the man matching the description was encountered, he should be detained, although how this was to be achieved was unspecified. One thing, though, was clear: the man with the green bicycle was the prime suspect. The police also appealed to bicycle repair shops for any information {see *Exhibit 4 for the full text of the handbill*}.

On the afternoon of Tuesday 8 July 1919, the inquest into the death of Bella Wright was opened by the coroner, Edmund Bouskell. The police were represented by Superintendent Levi Bowley and Chief Constable Edward Holmes. There were only two witnesses. Mary Ann Wright, Bella's mother, confirmed the identity of the dead girl, and Joseph Cowell confirmed that the body was the one he had discovered three days previously. The body was then released to the family for burial, and the inquest adjourned until Friday 25 July.

By Tuesday evening, the story of the cyclist's death had changed dramatically. The front page of the *Mercury* now ran the bold headline 'Stretton Murder Mystery' on the front page of a special edition. Bella Wright "was foully done to death on her way home after a spin around Evington… the police are searching for a man who was seen with the deceased on Saturday evening, and who is suspected of shooting her." It appears the editor had put two and two together to reach his own conclusion.

The reaction of the local newspapers would have significant repercussions later, but the report also brought immediate results for the police. A Leicester cycle dealer who had read the *Mercury* story came forward. Harry Cox informed Superintendent Bowley that only the previous week he had repaired the green bicycle described in the report. He had been instructed by the customer to adjust the three-speed gear control, a fault in which had made the bicycle almost unusable. During the work, Cox had accidentally broken the control cable, which he had to replace, extending the time the bicycle remained on his premises. Shortly after lunch on Saturday 5 July the customer had collected it, paying Cox four shillings and nine pence for his work.

Naturally, the police quizzed Cox about the green bicycle's owner. He confirmed to Superintendent Bowley that the customer matched the circulated description of the man – in particular, he was unshaven and had a squeaky voice with a cockney accent. What was his name? The man never gave his name, and Cox had no need to ask. Did he say where he lived? He did not, only that he worked in London and was in Leicester visiting friends while he was on leave. Anything else? The customer said he had been demobilised recently.

Although the police were confident that Cox's customer was the same man who left George Measure's cottage with Bella, the fact that the cyclist appeared to work in London spread the investigative net much further. Scotland Yard were contacted and now assisted in the inquiry. One of the detectives dispatched to Leicestershire was Chief Inspector Albert Hawkins. Later in the year, when the Metropolitan Police CID was reorganised into four areas, Hawkins became one of the 'big four' superintendents.

The interest in the 'murder mystery' extended beyond Leicester, with almost every newspaper giving the case coverage. In the afternoon of Friday 11 July 1919, Bella Wright was buried amid extraordinary scenes, with thousands of people lining the quiet lanes surrounding the spired St Mary's and All Saints church at Stoughton. The church pews were crammed, while hundreds stood solemnly outside to hear the vicar's sermon through the open porch doors. The address was notable because he spoke of Bella being "most foully murdered", reflecting the newspaper reports. Despite the absence of an inquest verdict, local people had made up their minds on how Bella had died. Mourners and untold numbers of onlookers filed past her final resting place, which overflowed with floral tributes including a heart-shaped wreath from her workmates at the mill. Kenus and Mary Wright retained their dignity throughout the occasion, but cannot have been comfortable with the overwhelming crowds intruding into their personal grief.

The police were present in great numbers, not only to ensure that the multitudes were orderly at the funeral but to search the crowd for anyone resembling the man last seen with Bella Wright. The search was fruitless. It was a harbinger of things to come. They were soon to discover that the man with the green bicycle had seemingly vanished into thin air.

Chapter 4

INTO THIN AIR

Following publication of the police handbill and newspaper reports of Bella Wright's death, the police interviewed anyone who might have known the deceased – friends, family and co-workers. They gleaned little useful information and nothing whatsoever concerning the identity of the man on the green bicycle. Archie Ward, Bella's informal fiancé, travelled from Portsmouth to answer police questions, but was quickly eliminated as a potential suspect. He mentioned that Bella had an ex-boyfriend who boasted that he had been intimate with Bella (which, it will be remembered, was consistent with the post mortem results). The previous boyfriend was traced, questioned, but also eliminated from the inquiry.

Bella's private life was not the only thing to be combed for clues. Local villagers were quizzed in the hope of discovering eyewitnesses who may have seen Bella or the man on the green bicycle. They had modest success – a few possible sightings – but nothing of significance. Not surprisingly, given its vagueness, the possible London connection yielded no results whatsoever. Leicestershire Constabulary had no hard leads. After only a week, the case appeared to be going cold.

Efforts were intensified to find the weapon. For two weeks a squad of police officers and farmers searched the local area. Dykes were cleaned, underbrush cleared, fields mowed. Nothing. Even without it, the lead investigators, Herbert Taylor and Levi Bowley, remained confident that the man on the green bicycle was the key to solving the case. Surely it was only a matter of time before a witness came forward to destroy the man's anonymity?

To aid the process, a second police handbill was published a week after the first. It again provided detailed descriptions of the man and his green bicycle, but contained some important differences {see *Exhibit 4*}. First, the reward for information leading to the identification of the man was increased to £20 – a significant sum, equivalent to £1,000 today. Second, the headline boldly proclaimed 'Murder At Stretton Parva'. This was a little premature – until the coroner delivered his verdict, the manner of death was officially unknown.

The second handbill raised the stakes, but was no more successful than the first. Despite intensive efforts by Leicestershire Constabulary, by the time the coroner's inquest resumed several weeks later, the case was no further forward. The second day of the inquest was held on Friday 25 July 1919 in the village hall of Great Glen, one of the larger villages in the locality, three miles to the south of Stoughton. The jury was told that two Scotland Yard detectives were helping Leicestershire Constabulary with its enquiries. The only witnesses were Dr Williams and Dr Phillips, who presented the findings of the autopsy. An important exchange occurred between Dr Williams and the coroner:

Coroner: Can you form any opinion as to the position of the girl when she was shot?
Williams: The shot must have been fired in an upwards direction.
Coroner: Can you say whether the girl was riding her bicycle when she was shot?
Williams: You cannot say. The girl may have been standing, but there are many possibilities; it is impossible to say.

Dr Williams conceded that he was not an expert on gunshot wounds, so his assertion that the shot must have been fired in an upwards direction is surprising. The position and angle of the victim's body at the time of impact is a crucial consideration when determining a bullet's angle of trajectory. As the doctor had no knowledge of these, his assertion that the shot was fired upwards appears to be unwarranted. Indeed, at the trial he would change his opinion.

The doctor also stated that surrounding the entrance wound he found minute particles of metal, but no traces of gunpowder. From this, he inferred that the victim had been shot from a distance of between four and five feet (less than two metres). This view appears to have been confirmed by a former police officer and amateur ballistics expert, who wrote to the police claiming that the tiny metal fragments would have been stripped from the bullet as it exited the muzzle of a revolver with a poorly aligned barrel and cylinder.

Another important exchange concerned a possible attack on Bella:

Coroner: Is there any evidence to show the girl had been assaulted prior to being shot?
Williams: No.
Coroner: Is there any evidence to show she had resisted any such attempt?
Williams: No, her clothes were not disarranged. She wore a bow, like girls do, and this was fastened by a flimsy pin, and this was intact.

Dr Phillips added that the lack of bruising on the victim's body confirmed, in his opinion, that there had been no struggle. However, the victim would not be expected to put up a fight if the putative assailant had a gun. Further, sexual assault can take many forms, including groping, which would not necessarily leave any physical evidence.

The inquest was adjourned again for two weeks. Chief Constable Holmes told the waiting press that he believed that someone knew something about the man with the green bicycle, who must have been living locally, and possibly still was, because he had visited a Leicester cycle shop. He stressed that the man could not be said to have committed murder, although the wording of the second handbill gave a different impression.

The penultimate day of the inquest was held on Friday 8 August 1919. Most of the witnesses were also called at the trial, which will be discussed later. One witness who was not was Bella's cousin, Margaret Evans, who told the coroner that Bella "had blushed" when approached by the man on the green bicycle. She believed that Bella and the man knew each other. {See Exhibit 5 for the inquest statements}.

A formal verdict of 'wilful murder' by person or persons unknown was returned. The coroner found it remarkable that no one had come forward to say they knew of a man who matched the description circulated by the police. The bicycle, in particular, was distinctive. He mused that a close relative might not be expected to give the fugitive away but, for the benefit of the gathered press reporting his words to the community, added that this could result in a charge of being an accessory to a crime.

Summer returned to England during the first half of August. After a six-week spell of generally unsettled and unseasonal weather, the atmospheric pressure and temperatures soared. People took advantage of the warm sunshine, and not only for leisure. Crops had to be harvested, and hops and fruits picked.

After a month of headlines and reports about the green bicycle murder, local newspapers turned their attention to other matters. After the inquest verdict, there were few stories about the mysterious shooting. By the time the weather turned again at the end of August, Bella Wright had been largely forgotten by the fickle press, which understandably focused on other matters, such as the Football League resuming after an absence of four years due to the war. Only Bella's family and friends continued to feel the void of her absence in their lives. They were left to grieve in private, away from the huge, prying crowds that had gathered for the funeral and the inquest.

The days shortened, autumn arrived. By October, cold, northerly winds blew across much of the country. Heavy and severe frosts were common as temperatures fell. By the end of the month, the leaves were falling. It could have been a metaphor for the Bella Wright case. The early optimism of detectives had been replaced by a stark realisation that her killer was unlikely to be brought to justice. Indeed, as early as mid-August, the Commissioner at Scotland Yard received a perfunctory letter from the office of the Director of Public Prosecutions:

I have read the papers in this case with considerable interest and am now returning them to you as I have little hope that the murderer will ever be caught.

Any chance of a prosecution depended on finding the enigmatic man on the green bicycle – and he had, seemingly, disappeared without a trace.

In December, the first Armistice was observed at the newly erected Cenotaph at Whitehall. A few weeks later Bella would have been interested to see Nancy Astor become the first woman to take her seat in the House of Commons. The election of a female Member of Parliament was merely a suffragette's dream before the war. Few thought they would see it happen so quickly. Weeks later, the Sex Disqualification (Removal) Act became law, opening up opportunities for women professionals for the first time. Ivy Williams soon became the first female student to be admitted to one of the Inns of Court, the exclusive associations for barristers and judges. These events signalled the beginning of a fundamental change in social attitudes in Britain that would become more pronounced in the decades to follow, in what should have been Bella's lifetime.

After the revelry of New Year's Eve, the decade changed and the so-called Roaring Twenties began. The case, however, was as cold and dull as the weather that swept across Britain in early January. For PC Alfred Hall, the memories of that night would stay with him until the day he died. He had not forgotten Bella, and occasionally he visited the lonely lane where she lost her life. Perhaps this homage was out of respect. Perhaps he clung to the hope that some clue might be revealed in the naked winter. But he had already played his part. Superintendents Taylor and Bowley feared that anyone who had any relevant information about the case would have come forward by now. Six months had slipped by, but it might as well have been six years. Without someone putting a name to the suspect's description, apprehending him was like looking for the proverbial needle. They needed something to chase down, to give the inquiry impetus. What happened next was certainly beyond their modest hopes for the case.

Enoch Whitehouse was a self-employed canal haulier, plying his usual trade on the River Soar, the waterway that winds its way through Leicester. On Monday 23 February 1920, he was delivering materials to St Mary's Mills, ironically the factory where Bella had worked. As his boat approached the wharf, his towrope slackened and fell into the water. About a minute later, as his boat manoeuvred, the rope tensioned again, lifting something out of the water. It appeared to be scrap metal snagged on the line. When the boat moved again, changing his vantage point, Whitehouse saw it was a bicycle frame. His surprise turned to delight when he noticed its colour: it was green.

As his barge neared the wharf, the rope slackened again and the bicycle frame fell back into the murky water. He noted the exact position where the canal had reclaimed its bounty. Later that day, Whitehouse started telling friends about his discovery, naturally keeping to himself its precise location. He rose early on Tuesday to stake his claim for the reward money. He was successful in retrieving it, although the bicycle was incomplete; the rear wheel and several parts were missing. News spread like wildfire. It was only fitting that the first to hear were the workers at St Mary's Mills, who excitedly poured out of the factory to glimpse the infamous green bicycle. It was on the towpath, propped up against a wall with Whitehouse proudly posing next to it like a big-game hunter.

By Friday the frame and front wheel of the bicycle had reached the office of Superintendent Levi Bowley. He recognised it as a BSA model – the type described by Jim Evans and printed on the handbills – and immediately contacted the manufacturers, who confirmed that the bicycle's unique serial number was required if there was to be any hope of tracing its owner. By Monday, the bicycle was in the hands of William Saunders, the Leicester agent for BSA Cycles.

The news was swift and bad. It was clear that the serial number stamped on the enamelled frame beneath the saddle had been carefully filed off. The detectives were confident that this was the bicycle they had been searching for; serial numbers are not scratched off unless there is something to hide. They quizzed Saunders. Was there only one serial number stamped on a bicycle? Typically, yes. The exception would be for a special order. Was this model special? It was impossible to tell without examining the entire bicycle. What about its unusual colour? It was not a common colour for a BSA bicycle but by no means special. The detectives feared they were at another dead end. Despondently, they left the machine with the dealer, who continued to examine the bicycle for anything that might help the police.

Piece by piece, Saunders dismantled the bicycle. When he removed the handlebar fork from the frame, he stumbled across some tiny characters stamped on the inside tube. He was sure this would be a manufacturer name, but as he looked under his magnifying glass he saw it was a serial number. Clearly, the bicycle had been a special order. It was a massive stroke of luck for the police. Within an hour Superintendent Bowley held a piece of paper on which a six-digit number had been carefully printed: 103648. He punched the air in jubilation. It was like finding a lost combination code for a safe full of riches.

After months of being starved of leads, Leicestershire Constabulary now pounced like a hungry lynx. The next morning Superintendent Taylor headed to the offices of Birmingham Small Arms Company, the arms manufacturer and parent company of BSA Cycles, at Redditch, Worcestershire. Taylor was directed to the office of clerk Albert Davis, who heaved several large ledgers onto his desk. Having looked at the serial number he thought a good starting year would be 1916, but one by one the years were put aside. With each discarded volume, Taylor became increasingly anxious. A few moments later, however, Davis jabbed the ledger triumphantly with his finger, announcing that order number 103648 had been placed on 3 May 1910. A mightily relieved Taylor noted down the date. Running his finger across the columns of the neatly handwritten ledger, the clerk provided further details. The special order was for a deluxe bicycle with a pedal rim brake fitted to the rear wheel. And then the crucial information – it was dispatched to a dealer called Orton Brothers in Derby.

On returning to Leicester later that day, Taylor made further enquiries. To his relief, Orton Brothers was still trading. On Wednesday morning he and a colleague took the train to Derby. They were greeted by Joseph Orton, one of the firm's partners. Would Orton Brothers have records from 10 years ago? Luckily, they did. Orton found the entry for serial number 103648. It had been a special order, he told Taylor, based on the specification of the customer. It had been priced at 13 pounds and 13 shillings, equivalent to £1,500 today. The customer had paid in cash. Who was the buyer? Mr Ronald Light. Was there an address? Yes. In fact, there were two.

Taylor and his colleague lost no time in visiting both Derby addresses, but they were hardly surprised to learn that Ronald Light no longer resided at either. Their luck held when a lodger at one of the addresses remembered the man and his green bicycle. Like joining the numbers in a dot-to-dot puzzle, the detectives followed a chain of addresses until they had caught up with their elusive pimpernel. As suspected from the beginning, the man they sought had lived in Leicester at the time of the shooting, but he was now living in Cheltenham. They moved quickly to make an arrest.

Members of the Cold Case Jury, in the following reconstruction we encounter Ronald Light for the first time. It is the morning of Thursday 4 March 1920. The place is Dean Close School, Cheltenham. Superintendent Herbert Taylor has travelled there to question and detain Ronald Light.

"Dr William Flecker at your service, gentlemen," announced the distinguished-looking man, dressed in a dark suit with a large clerical collar. "Welcome to Dean Close." The headmaster shook hands enthusiastically with Herbert Taylor and an accompanying local sergeant, before ushering them into his study. "Can I offer you a cup of Darjeeling?" he asked, reclining in his captain's chair.

"Any tea would be welcome," Taylor replied. Dr Flecker looked at his secretary, who nodded and closed the study door.

"Pray, what can I do for you?"

"I believe Mr Ronald Light is a tutor here," Taylor said.

"Indeed, he is, yes. He's our junior mathematical and science master. He started with us only the month before last. I interviewed him myself for the post."

"When was that, sir?"

"Oh, it was some time before Christmas."

"Can you be more specific?"

Flecker looked down at his diary, turning a few pages. "It

would have been the first week in December."

"He replied to an advertisement, did he?"

"He wrote to us about the position and I interviewed him the same week. He had very satisfactory references. A jolly good thing, too! There's an awful shortage of tutors in the country. So many were slaughtered in..." Flecker closed his eyes as his voiced tailed off. He was not only thinking of the large numbers of would-be teachers killed during the war, but the scores of former pupils that had also perished. He had recently learned the final death toll had been over a hundred. Even for a man of his strong faith, he found it difficult to divine any purpose to losing so much talent and potential. He composed himself. "We are grateful when Providence sends us good staff, gentlemen."

"And when did he commence his duties here?"

"Let me see... that would be on the 20th of the month before last."

"January?"

"Yes."

Taylor jotted the date in his notebook. "And, if I may ask, how have you found him?"

"A true gentleman, I would say, and a jolly good tutor. He's so enthusiastic in all his duties, and he's already involved himself in the outdoor pursuits of the boys. Given his war experience, I've put him in charge of the school armoury." Taylor arched an eyebrow. "He's in class at the moment. Can this wait? I'm sure this cannot be anything serious, Superintendent." Like a seasoned politician, Flecker flashed a congenial smile from underneath his greying paintbrush moustache.

"I'm afraid it is, Headmaster," Taylor replied solemnly.

"Oh, I see." The headmaster was already alarmed at the potential damage to the reputation of the private school. It had just nine boarders when he was appointed as its first headmaster in the 1880s. Thanks to his dedication, it now boasted over two hundred, and a growing reputation for athletic as well as academic excellence. With a national shortage of tutors, however, the last thing Dean Close needed was a scandal involving one of its masters. "You may conduct your interview in my study, if that is convenient." He hoped this would keep the matter discreet, at least for the time being.

"Thank you. And we will need to search his room. I assume he has lodgings here?"

"Yes, of course." He stood up. "I will fetch him for you personally."

The headmaster left. Shortly afterwards, the tea arrived. As they sipped their drinks, the two police officers admired the beautifully furnished study with views over expansive playing fields.

"What does that mean?" the sergeant asked, nodding toward the large school crest on the wall.

"Verbum Dei Lucerna," Taylor read aloud. "The word of God, a light." He took a sip of tea. "I think that means a guiding light, like a lamp or a torch."

"I wish God could guide us occasionally," the sergeant joked.

"The evidence is our lamp, Sergeant."

The study door opened and the detectives rose from their chairs. Dr Flecker, accompanied by a small, smartly dressed man, entered the room. Taylor studied his quarry for the first time. Ronald Light was wearing a jacket and waistcoat on which hung a gold watch and chain. Sharply ironed trousers broke on gleaming black shoes. His hair, brown and flecked with grey, was neatly cut and he was clean shaven.

"I'll be waiting outside, gentlemen. Please let me know when you are done, or if there is anything else you require." Flecker withdrew, closing the door behind him.

"Can I help you?" Light asked in a squeaky voice. He was invited to sit. Taking a cigarette from his jacket pocket, he asked "May I?" Without waiting for an answer, he lit it. After a few puffs, he placed the cigarette in the corner of his mouth. Observing Light keenly, Taylor thought this behaviour showed great social confidence. The man was from a middle-class background and well educated, he surmised.

"You are Mr Ronald Light, I presume?"

"I am," he replied, without removing the cigarette.

"Ronald Vivian Light?"

"Yes."

"My name is Herbert Taylor. I'm a detective superintendent with Leicestershire Constabulary. I have a few questions to ask you in connection with the death of Bella Wright in Leicestershire last year."

"I see," Light replied casually.

Taylor took another sip of tea, the bone china cup clinking as he replaced it on the saucer. "Last year, were you living at 54 Highfield Street, Leicester?"

"I was. It is my mother's house and I had a room there."

"Were you living there last July?"

"I was, certainly."

"Where were you on 5 July 1919 at approximately 9pm?"

"I have no idea, sir," Light shot back. He looked at the two detectives individually. "Can you say where you were at that precise date and time?"

"Perhaps you could think about where you might have been?"

Light removed the cigarette from his mouth, rolling it gently between his thumb and forefinger. "I expect I was at home. My mother likes to take dinner at 8pm."

"So you do have some idea where you might have been," Taylor remarked dryly. "Are you sure you were not near Gaulby at that time?"

"Gaulby? I don't think I've heard of the place."

"It's a small village a few miles to the east of Leicester. Perhaps you've been there?"

Light shrugged his shoulders. "If I have, I don't remember."

"Have you ever spoken to Bella Wright?"

"No, I don't think so."

Taylor passed him a photograph, but after a cursory glance Light returned it. "You don't recognise this girl?" the superintendent enquired. "Perhaps you would care to take a longer look?" He returned the photograph to Light who looked at the image for a few moments, taking a puff of his cigarette. "Oh, I seem to remember seeing her picture in the papers last year," he said coolly. "That's all."

Taylor took back the photograph and changed tack. "Have you ever owned a green bicycle?"

"No."

"You have never bought a green BSA bicycle?"

Chapter 4

"No."

"Are you sure?"

"As certain as you're sitting before me."

Taylor knew he was dealing with a clever, quick-witted and resourceful character, but he was equal to his task. "Are you saying that you never bought a green BSA bicycle from Orton Brothers in Derby?"

Wrong-footed, Light fell silent for the first time. Checking his notebook, Taylor delivered his coup de grace. "That would have been in May 1910."

Buying some time, Light sent a plume of smoke into the room. "Now you mention it, I did buy a green bicycle, I think, when I lived in Derby. I don't remember the dealer, though. I had forgotten all about it because I sold it about a year later. I've owned so many bicycles over the years."

"To whom did you sell it?"

"I can't remember the gentlemen's name," Light retorted, trying to regain the upper hand. "It was so many years ago, you know, before the war."

Taylor drank the last of his tea. "Mr Cox can identify the man who took the green bicycle to his shop." He closed his notebook, placing it in his inside jacket pocket. Standing up, he said: "Mr Light, I am not satisfied with your answers. I am requesting that you accompany me to Cheltenham police station."

"What is this stunt?" Light remonstrated. "I have classes to teach. It's trigonometry this afternoon."

Despite his protestations, Ronald Light accompanied Taylor to the police station. Henry Cox, the Leicester bicycle repairer, was already there, having being summoned to Cheltenham. At the station, a line-up of men wearing various suits and hats had already been assembled. Light, wearing his flat cap, was the smallest and joined the procession of faces. Cox was invited to view it.

Reading from a piece of paper, a burly officer asked Cox: "Did any of these men enter your shop on Saturday 5 July 1919 to collect a green bicycle?"

Henry Cox took one look down the line and without hesitation pointed to a man. "That one."

"The fourth one from the left?"

"Yes."

"Are you sure?"

"It's definitely him. No question."

The officer asked Ronald Light to step forward while the other members of the line-up were ushered away. "That man had me spotted, all right," Light commented casually. "Do you have a cigarette?" The officer was taken aback by the suspect's sangfroid.

Superintendent Taylor approached. "Ronald Vivian Light..."

"I think it was Charles Bourne of Derby," Light interjected calmly. "The chap I sold the bicycle to."

"You sold a green BSA bicycle to a Mr Charles Bourne?"

"Yes. It's not the only bicycle I've sold. It's not a crime is it?"

Taylor ignored the rhetorical question. "Ronald Vivian Light, I am arresting you on suspicion of murdering Annie Bella Wright. You are not obliged to say anything unless you wish to, but anything you say will be written down and may be used in evidence." Taylor savoured each word of the caution, as if he were reciting a favourite poem. After all the waiting and dead-ends, the elusive man on the green bicycle was in custody.

"Have you anything to say?"

Light remained silent. It was a sign of things to come.

Members of the Cold Case Jury, first impressions count. To Detective Superintendent Taylor, Ronald Light appeared remarkably cool and unfazed for someone who was obviously lying. His self-assurance was shot through with a disturbing narcissism. Even if this is correct, however, you should not yet infer that Light is guilty of anything, let alone murder. You will recall that within days of the body's discovery the press were reporting that Bella Wright had been murdered. The second police handbill requested information regarding the 'Murder at Stretton'. The reverend at Bella's funeral said she had been "most foully murdered". Under these circumstances, someone who had innocently cycled home with Bella on the night she died might have denied doing so for fear of being wrongly implicated in a capital crime. As you will see shortly, this would be in keeping with his character.

In further identity parades Ronald Light was identified by George Measures and Jim Evans. Both were adamant that the man in the line-up was the one who had left the cottage with Bella. Measures was so certain that, as he pointed to Light in the line-up, he shouted, "That's the man I want!" The police had found their prime suspect, but who was he?

Ronald Vivian Light was born in Leicester on 19 October 1885. He was the only son of George Light, a colliery manager, and his wife Catherine, who was from a wealthy solicitor's family. Their son had a privileged start to life.

When he was 11 he was sent to a prep school and, two years later, he was a pupil at Oakham, one of two private schools in Leicester at the time. He did not finish his education there, however. He was expelled at 17 years old for inappropriate behaviour with a much younger pupil, the official reason being that he had lifted a girl's clothes over her head. Expulsion from such a school was a disgrace for the family.

Light continued his education at the City and Guilds College, London, before accepting an engineering apprenticeship with Midland Railway at Derby. Light completed his apprenticeship when he was 25 years old, becoming an engineering assistant with the company. Four years later history repeated itself: Light misbehaved and was dismissed. It appears that he set fire to a store cupboard, but there were also rumours that he had been caught writing crude graffiti on lavatory walls. Either way, for a 29-year-old man, Ronald Light appears to have had a puerile side to his character. Nevertheless, there is no indication that he was violent. In fact, he was well-liked by his colleagues.

Light was fired from Midland Railway in October 1914, when the gathering storms of war had finally broken over Europe. Ever resourceful, he told friends that he had quit his job to enlist. He did, but only four months later, perhaps waiting to assess the truth of proclamations that the war would be over by Christmas.

He was posted as a second lieutenant in the Royal Engineers, a position for which he was well qualified. For the next six months he trained with the corps at Buxton, Derbyshire, and he was sent on active duty to France in

November 1915. He served as an officer for 10 weeks as the army prepared the ground for the Somme offensive the following year. He was deployed constructing and maintaining the trenches, sometimes at the Front.

The pattern of Light's career continued: after less than 10 weeks of active service, Light was dismissed and sent back to Britain. The official reason – that he lacked the initiative to make an efficient officer – is puzzling. Surely, the army could have demoted him but still retained his valuable services? In *The Green Bicycle Murder* (1993), Wendy East records that there was a persistent rumour that Light had assaulted a French postmistress while off duty. Light was stripped of his commission on 1 July 1916. Back in France, it was the first day of the massive Somme offensive, the worst day in British military history, which resulted in 60,000 casualties. We do not know how Light felt at being cashiered, but one wonders whether he was quietly pleased to be home regardless of the circumstances. His father, however, was distraught and anxious. Not long after his son's dismissal, he fell from an open second-floor window, suffering fatal injuries. The coroner found insufficient evidence as to the manner of his death. He appeared to have fainted, yet suicide could not be ruled out.

Ronald spent the summer of 1916 farm labouring in the West Country. It must have been infinitely preferable to fighting at the Somme. In September, perhaps due to growing peer pressure, he enlisted for a second time, this time as a gunner with the Honourable Artillery Company. Light was part of its reserve battery and remained in London when the Company sailed for France in April 1917.

According to East, in early May, an order was received to ready the reserve battery to join the Company. The following day a telegram from the War Office cancelled the order. A few weeks later, the mobilising order was received again. Incredibly, several days later, a telegram from Lord Denbigh, the commanding officer of the Honourable Artillery Company, rescinded the order for a second time.

The War Office quickly discovered something was amiss when Lord Denbigh demanded to know why the reserve battery was not already in France. Many men of the reserve battery were forced to sit a handwriting examination. Experts concluded that the telegrams had been sent by Gunner Ronald Light. Light knew the reason behind the tests, and surely he had the wits to disguise his handwriting, so why did he not do so? Is it possible he preferred the likely punishment – imprisonment – to being sent on active service? Or did he fear being arrested by French authorities for the putative assault on the postmistress had he returned? If so, his plan worked. A district court martial found him guilty of forging telegraphic orders and sentenced him to one year's detention. If he thought he could see out the rest of the war in safe disgrace, he was mistaken. Light was released after serving only a third of his sentence and was sent to France in November 1917.

Light saw 10 months of active duty, but by August 1918 he was a patient at a military hospital in Sheffield suffering from "progressive deafness, associated with ringing noises in both ears". Three months later the war ended. In February 1919, Light was demobilised and lived with his mother in Leicester. Unemployed but kept by his doting mother, he remained there for almost a year, only leaving when he secured the teaching position at Dean Close School. Given his career, one wonders how he managed to secure references for such a post. His mother's connections might have helped or, with his audacious ability for deceit, perhaps he had no need to rely on the genuine opinions of others.

It is fair to say Ronald Light did not have a distinguished army career. Indeed, many members of the Cold Case Jury may infer he was an unsavoury and untrustworthy character. This might be true, but it does not indicate that he was guilty of a cold-blooded murder. Indeed, Light seems to have gone to great lengths to avoid conflict, at least when his own well-being was at stake. What is certain is that he was extremely resourceful in serving his own interests and he was prepared to be deceitful on a breathtaking scale. By itself, however, this only shows that if Light believed his interests were best served by denying any connection with Bella Wright, he would have little compunction in doing so and with an aplomb few could equal.

Yet, despite his undoubted intelligence and resourcefulness, Ronald Light was in custody and facing a charge of murder.

Chapter 5

THE GREAT DEFENDER

On 5 March 1920, Ronald Light was brought before a local magistrate and formally charged with the wilful murder of Bella Wright. He was remanded in custody.

While Light waited for the committal hearing to commence, which would determine whether the prosecution had a strong enough case to send him for trial on the charge of murder, the police stepped up their activities. On Tuesday 9 March, statements were taken from two young girls. They claimed that, on the evening of Saturday 5 July 1919, a man on a green bicycle had approached them as they cycled near Leicester. He had tried to separate the girls, wanting to ride alone with just one of them. Sensibly, the girls had stuck together and rode home. The police arranged a line-up of Ronald Light and nine other men. They both picked out Ronald Light as the man who had approached them. Light was later to complain that he had not been allowed to shave, and this was the reason he was picked out by the girls, who distinctly recalled that the man

Chapter 5

was unshaven.

After the frame of the green bicycle had been plucked from the River Soar, an extensive dredging operation began. The police were interested in discovering whether a revolver had also been dumped in the canal. Every day for nearly six weeks the towpaths were packed with excited spectators who watched men fish the canal with rakes, poles and nets. Day after day an array of items was brought to the surface, a large handcart transporting them back to police headquarters for inspection. Plenty of dropped barge coal was salvaged and quickly bagged by shrewd bystanders. Systematically, the trawling teams moved further downstream from where the bicycle frame had been found. Eventually, their persistence was rewarded.

On Friday 12 March, a rear wheel was recovered and matched to the green bicycle. It was not proof in itself but demonstrated that Light had dismantled the bicycle and dumped various parts over a wide section of the canal. Expectations were raised. They were met a week later when a brown leather army revolver holster was fished out. It contained treasure: wrapped inside were nearly two dozen .455 cartridges – the same calibre as the bullet found by PC Hall. When Light heard about the recovery he was reported to have cursed in his cell: "Damn and blast that canal!" If this is true, it was the only time he ever lost his composure.

Huge crowds gathered in expectation of witnessing the revolver being hoisted from the water but, despite intensive search efforts, it was never found. However, the back-brake pedalling mechanism was recovered. It was not significant, except symbolically: it was the presence of this device that warranted the second serial number on the green bicycle, without which Ronald Light would never have been traced.

On Wednesday 24 March, after hearing testimony over two consecutive days, the magistrate concluded that there was a prima facie case to be presented to a jury. Ronald Light was invited to make a statement. "I am innocent and, on the advice of my legal advisers, I reserve my defence." He was committed to stand trial at the next assize.

The committal hearing had revealed the prosecution's hand. This was in stark contrast to the defence, which had been virtually mute. Ronald Light had made no statement and the defence team asked few questions in cross-examination, certainly none that indicated Light had changed his attitude of denying the circumstantial evidence that pointed to his guilt. In the press, speculation was mounting as to how a successful defence could possibly be brought. Unless Light had an alibi he looked doomed, and he would certainly need a good lawyer. Light's mother was well aware of this and, after receiving financial assistance from a wealthy friend, did not hire merely a good defence barrister, but the finest in the country. Indeed, some would consider Sir Edward Marshall Hall among the best defence barristers to have ever stepped into criminal court. Not only that, Marshall Hall would later say that his defence of Light was his best ever performance.

'The Great Defender', as he was known when he represented Light, was blessed with the holy trinity of attributes for a barrister: physical presence, charisma and oratory. Tall, broad, and serenely featured with an expressive voice, he was an Adonis of an advocate. He possessed a generous, bright personality and a high intelligence. A master of persuasion, he was able to obtain the most precious prize for any defendant: a jury's sympathy.

His secret in connecting with a jury was empathy. This was due to an intense sensitivity that had been heightened by pain and suffering during his life. His greatest tragedy was love. He loved with passion, and his pain must have been deep when, in the honeymoon carriage, his newly wedded wife, Ethel (née Moon), told him that she had never loved him in the way he loved her. One can only speculate why she married him – perhaps it was due to love's imposters, admiration and kindness – but she felt imprisoned from the moment she made her vows. Not surprisingly, the marriage was doomed. Although he never ceased to care for her – as he had done from his childhood – he realised their union would never escape the long shadow of unhappiness it cast. Six years later, although legally still married, they formally separated.

This was not the end of the story. She fell passionately in love with a young officer, became pregnant, and secretly underwent an abortion by a backstreet doctor. It was horrendously botched. As she lay wracked with remorse, as well as pain, she asked for her husband, who without hesitation rushed to be by her side. Perhaps in those dark, painful hours she realised the meaning and value of true love. If she had, her husband never heard the words he longed to hear: she died before he could reach her. It was the final betrayal of a forlorn first love.

This was not the only setback. The following year his

mother, to whom he was devoted, died. Then in 1895, after contracting double pneumonia, he lost his robust health, but not his optimistic and confident spirit. This was nearly crushed five years later, however, when he was severely censured by senior judges for his tactics during a libel trial against the *Daily Mail*. Marshall Hall had won the case emphatically: the jury awarded considerable damages, equivalent to £250,000 today, and over double that demanded by the plaintiff. The appeal claimed that Marshall Hall's closing speech was a vituperative and unfair attack on the newspaper that had inflamed the jury. In particular, he had made comments that had impugned the reputation of the newspaper proprietor's wife, which had enraged the proprietor far more than the damages. The appeal judges ruled that Marshall Hall's "monstrous" and "disgraceful" comments were indefensible and inadmissible. Every major newspaper reported his reprimand, with *The Times* carrying the headline: "Counsel censured: verdict obtained by such means cannot stand."

After the tragedy in his personal life, the censure savaged his reputation and brought him to the edge of ruin. It took several years of hard work to recover, mainly through brilliant defences in prominent criminal trials in which he always empathised with his client. Unlike many in his profession, he appreciated how easily people can mis-step and be swept along by misfortune. Combining extensive technical knowledge with razor-sharp argument and powerful oratory, his virtuoso performances in court were theatrical as well as effective. When he defended Light, Marshall Hall's fame was unsurpassed by any lawyer in the country.

Chapter 5

On Wednesday 9 June 1920, the trial of Ronald Light for the murder of Bella Wright began in the cramped court-room at Leicester Castle. It is a scandal that there is no trial transcript. We only have newspaper accounts of the proceedings, but this is like having a heavily pixelated image when you desire the detail of a high-resolution photograph. Nevertheless, from these accounts I have provided minutes of the trial, including a brief summary of every witness state-ment {Exhibit 7}, and pieced together some of the exchanges in court.

The trial is extraordinary in that Marshall Hall accepted the prosecution's case against his client apart from several key points. There was no disputing that Light owned the green bicycle and later disposed of it, or that he had cycled with Bella Wright on the night she died. Marshall Hall knew that these facts were irrefutable. If Light attempted to deny them it would be evident that he was committing perjury. Marshall Hall knew all too well that a jury would never acquit a barefaced liar.

The defence case had three objectives. Marshall Hall wanted to shake the evidence of the two young girls who claimed to have met Light; to refute any suggestion that Light knew Bella; and, most importantly, to undermine the ballistics evidence that pointed to Bella having been killed by an army service revolver. Let us examine these disputed aspects of the case in turn.

The first task was to question the young girls who alleged that Light had approached them. Marshall Hall was worried that the jury would consider any such approach by a much older man unusual, even disturbing, and might also suggest to the jury that Light had similarly approached Bella Wright hours later. His cross-examination of the girls was gentle, his voice low and soft, but effective. Here is part of the cross-examination of 14-year-old Muriel Nunney:

Counsel: Did you hear about the so-called 'green bicycle case'?

Nunney: Yes, sir.

Counsel: You saw the photographs and read about it in the papers, I suppose?

Nunney: Yes.

Counsel: You were asked by the police whether you had seen this particular man on 5 July?

Nunney: Yes, sir.

Counsel: They gave you the date?

Nunney: Yes.

Counsel (to the judge): I would point out that the two girls were not called upon to give statements to the police until 9 March 1920; statements of something said to have occurred on 5 July 1919.

Marshall Hall had achieved his objective effortlessly. The girls' statements were given only after Light's arrest; they had read about the case prior to giving their statements; and they had also been led by the suggestion of the date on which they might have seen him. This so weakened the probative value of the testimony that, in his summing up, the judge directed the jury to ignore the girls' evidence. During his testimony, Light denied not only seeing the girls on 5 July but that he had ever seen them on any occasion.

Chapter 5

The cross-examination of George Measures was equally important to the defence. Bella's uncle had testified that Light, when he appeared outside the cottage, had said "Bella, you have been a long time." This suggested that Light knew the victim, something the accused had consistently denied. Further, it was easier for the prosecution to suggest that Light had murdered Bella if he had known her – even a century ago it was known that a woman was less likely to be murdered by a complete stranger. Two questions were all Marshall Hall needed to make his point.

Counsel: Might the accused have said, "Hello, you have been a long time"?
Measures: No, he said "Bella".
Counsel: Did you not ask your niece whether she knew the man, and did she not reply, "I do not know the man, he is a perfect stranger to me"?
Measures: Yes.

Jim Evans also testified that Light had said, "Bella, you have been a long time." It was left to the judge to seek clarification.
Judge: Do you think the prisoner said "Hello" or "Bella" to the deceased?
Evans: It was "Bella", your Lordship.

Marshall Hall was unconcerned by his answer. Having plundered the testimony of the previous witness, there was no need to cross-examine. The prize, of course, was that Bella herself had said that she did not know the accused. This small detail was sufficient for the barrister to make a big point in his closing speech to the jury:

The victim had said the accused was a perfect stranger to her. Why was this evidence not to be accepted as much as the other evidence? That Light did not know the girl was not contradicted... The only evidence to support the belief that the man knew her was a casual conversation... Upon this flimsy statement you are being asked to find that two people were known one to the other.

Of course, this makes a convenient assumption: that Bella had told the truth to her uncle. If she had felt uncomfortable by the appearance of Light and what her uncle might have thought about her acquaintance with such a man, she might have denied knowing him. Such shades of grey are not the concern of barristers, however, who deal only in the black and white of verdicts.

The defence had won some minor skirmishes, yet the looming battle was over the ballistics. Dr Williams had testified about the medical evidence, restating his autopsy findings. On being shown the .455 calibre bullet found in the road near the deceased, Williams stated that the wounds could have been caused by the exhibited bullet. This was the battle line. The .455 calibre bullet was the putative cause of death and was linked, albeit circumstantially, to the accused through the identical rounds dredged from the canal.

Marshall Hall first questioned the expertise of Dr Williams.

Counsel: Do you have much experience of gunshot wounds?
Williams: No, I cannot say I have.

Williams had earlier stated the same thing at the

committal hearing and urged that an expert forensic pathologist was required. This request had been ignored – an error, not least because Marshall Hall was an expert on firearms. Perhaps to atone for his lack of knowledge, Dr Williams showed the court the jar of formalin containing the excised skin from Bella's cheek. The ghoulish exhibit did not faze Marshall Hall, who carefully removed the skin from the jar. He showed that his slim pencil barely fitted through the puncture: it was a small entrance wound. Although larger, the described exit wound was also small. The cross-examination continued.

Counsel: Do you know for what distance a service revolver will throw a bullet?
Williams: I'm not sure.
Counsel: Would you be surprised to learn it is more than half a mile?
Williams. No, that doesn't surprise me.
Counsel: At what distance do you believe the firearm was discharged?
Williams: No more than six to seven feet.

A bullet's velocity is greatest as it leaves the muzzle. Consequently, a bullet fired from close range is travelling at near maximum velocity. The destructive power of a bullet is proportional to its size and velocity, and other things being equal, the tissue damage caused by a high velocity impact is greater. Hence, a bullet fired from close range tends to inflict more serious injuries. Marshall Hall used these facts to frame his next question.

Counsel: Do you not think that a bullet at this size travelling at tremendous velocity would leave a larger exit wound?

Williams: No, I don't think so.

Counsel: Do you not agree that the clean entrance hole indicates a high velocity bullet?

Williams: I think so, yes.

Counsel: Then how do you get out of this dilemma? A bullet fired upwards and travelling at such velocity is only found six yards from the body.

Williams: I believe the bullet may have hit stony ground underneath her head and have retained sufficient momentum to take it into the road.

Counsel: But that theory is only tenable on the assumption that the woman was on the ground, is it not?

Williams: Of course.

Counsel: Yet, you told the coroner that you could not form an opinion as to the position of the woman when she was shot, did you not?

Williams. I have thought about the matter a great deal since.

Counsel: Then you agree that, without further resistance, it is absurd to suggest that the bullet came to rest only six yards away?

Williams: I suppose so, yes.

Marshall Hall's questioning of Dr Williams prepared the ground for his attack on the prosecution's ballistic evidence. This came during his cross-examination of the next expert witness, Henry Clarke, a local gunsmith who had confirmed that the bullet found by PC Hall was a .455 calibre adapted for army service revolvers and identical to the bullets retrieved from the canal. The following testimony is an abridged account of the exchanges between the defence barrister and the gunsmith.

Counsel: Would you agree that this bullet has been manufactured in its hundreds of millions?

Clarke: I cannot say how many of these cartridges were made.

Counsel: The bullet was standard issue as long ago as the Boer War. Do you disagree that hundreds of millions must have been made?

Clarke: I cannot disagree.

Counsel (taking out a magnifying glass and examining the bullet): Would you agree that this bullet shows marks indicating that it has been fired through a rifled barrel?

Clarke (examining the bullet): Yes, sir.

Counsel: This bullet might then just as easily have been fired from a rifle as well as a revolver?

Clarke: Yes.

Counsel: How far might a bullet fired from a service revolver travel?

Clarke: At least a thousand yards.

Counsel: We are told the exit wound in this poor girl's head was an oval, one-and-a-half inches by half-an-inch. Is that an unusually small exit wound to be made by a bullet of this size?

Clarke: No, sir.

Counsel: If the bullet had been fired at a distance of six or seven feet from the metalled road, would you expect to find the bullet in the condition as this one?

Clarke: Yes, if it struck the road at an angle.

Counsel: Have you seen a human being who has been shot at a distance of within five yards with a service revolver?

Clarke: No, sir.

Counsel: I suggest that the effect of such a bullet on the skull is almost to blow the side of the head off.

Clarke: It depends on the velocity.

Marshall Hall's argument was that if the bullet that allegedly killed Bella Wright had been fired from close range, as Dr Williams claimed, then (a) the bullet would not have been found so close to the body; and (b) the wounds would have been more severe. There is a rebuttal to the first point. The bullet might have fallen much further along the road only to be dragged back by traffic or cattle to where it was found. When re-examined by the prosecution, Clarke stated that a badly worn revolver barrel would diminish the velocity and penetrating force of a bullet fired from it, a counter to the second point. The judge then posed a question.

Judge: Do you see anything inconsistent in the condition of the bullet with its having passed through the head of the dead woman, and then having its course arrested by the turf where it joins the metalled edge of the road and landing 17 feet away?

Clarke: No.

In *The Green Bicycle Case*, Russell Wakefield says:
The evidence pointed most emphatically to the fact that

Bella Wright was shot while lying on her back in the road. On no other assumption can the discovery of the bullet be explicable.

This is mistaken. While the expert testimony gave some support to the view that Bella Wright was shot at close range while she was prostrate on the road, Marshall Hall had disputed it vehemently. In his closing speech he stated that he had "never heard such ridiculous evidence to suggest that a lead bullet fired into the ground would bounce into the air at right angles and then fall to the ground". Furthermore, there is an alternative explanation for the bullet's position in the road: it was a coincidence and unconnected to the case. Marshall Hall was convinced that the spent .455 calibre bullet was already lying in the road when Bella Wright was shot dead. He did not vigorously advance this position in court but, in a letter to a friend after the trial, he wrote:

The coincidence of the bullet was literally astounding, as I am convinced the bullet that was found within 17 feet of the body never killed the girl; but the deadly thing was that the accused man had in his possession at the time identical bullets. True, I elicited in cross-examination, they are made in thousands of millions, but for all that it was a coincidence.

Wakefield scoffs at this suggestion: "Surely it is the zenith of coincidence if a dead body and a bullet were found within a few yards of each other in a placid Midland lane, and the two in no way connected." To which it might be added: and the bullet also be identical to those discarded by the accused.

Had Marshall Hall's fabled expertise in firearms failed him? Before the trial he had fired a .455 Webley & Scott revolver to assess its destructive power. Used by the military services, its typical bullet was three times heavier than the ammunition used in smaller calibre weapons, and was designed to stop a man dead in his tracks. After his experiments he concluded that it was impossible for Bella Wright to have been killed by such a powerful firearm from close range. If she had, her head would have been blown apart and the bullet would have travelled much further. Accepting this, his logic followed the famous dictum of Sherlock Holmes: having eliminated the impossible, whatever remains – even the zenith of coincidence – is the truth.

To support his view, Marshall Hall asked a renowned ballistics expert of the day to examine the bullet, but the barrister did not receive the answer he expected. Robert Churchill was adamant that its distinctive grooves and twists showed it could have been fired only from a Webley & Scott revolver. Not surprisingly, Marshall Hall did not call Churchill to testify for the defence, nor was he called by the prosecution {see *Exhibit 8 for further details*}.

Is there any support for Marshall Hall's contention? The autopsy report {*Exhibit 3*} stated that the entrance wound "admitted an ordinary lead pencil". This suggests that its size was very similar to a pencil's diameter, which is approximately 0.28" (7mm). The diameter of the bullet found by PC Hall was significantly larger – 0.45" (11.5mm). The size of the entrance wound appears to be more consistent with smaller calibre firearms, such as a .32 revolver or a .30 rook rifle, which have bullets matching a pencil's diameter. Despite this, it should be stressed that both the doctor and gunsmith saw no inconsistency between the exhibited bullet and the inflicted wounds. Indeed, PC Hall testified that "one could comfortably insert a lead pencil" into the entrance wound, suggesting its diameter might have been larger. Presumably this was also the opinion of Dr Williams, who conceded at the earlier committal hearing that the .455 calibre bullet was thicker than an ordinary pencil yet still maintained it could have caused the wounds.

The large calibre bullet was central to the prosecution's case. Any doubt that it was the cause of death would break the critical chain of circumstantial evidence against Light, and Marshall Hall would be able to show there was reasonable doubt. Yet the famous barrister was keenly aware that the jurors would ask one question repeatedly in their deliberations: if Light was innocent, why did he cover his tracks and remain silent? Worse, when he did say something, why did he lie? Surely these actions point to only one thing – guilt. Marshall Hall now faced one of his sternest tests as an advocate. Everything would rest on how Ronald Light told his story for the first time.

Chapter 6

BREAKING THE SILENCE

During the early stages of the trial, Light wrote an instruction for his barrister:

Will you please ask me to tell the jury in my own words exactly why I did not come forward? I will say I was dreadfully worried, and for some days was quite dazed at such an unexpected blow, and could not think clearly. When I began to think, I could not make up my mind to come forward, and hesitated for days. I could not give the police any information whatsoever as to how the girl met her death. If the police and papers had only stated the known facts, and asked the cyclist to come forward, I would have done so, but they jumped to the wrong conclusion, and I was frightened when I saw I was wanted for murder. Let me do this in my own words.

Marshall Hall was greatly relieved for two reasons. First, it was clear from the instructions that his client was intelligent and articulate. Second, in breaking the silence that he had kept since his arrest, Light was not denying ownership of the green bicycle, nor that he was the last man seen with

Chapter 6

Bella. The Great Defender now believed that, with his client's testimony, he had a chance of securing an acquittal.

Based on newspaper reports and secondary sources, the following is an abridged account of the exchanges between Marshall Hall and Ronald Light. Among the first questions were several about the revolver Light said he had owned.

Counsel: Have you ever possessed a revolver?
Light: Yes.
Counsel: Where did you get it from?
Light: I bought it from my commanding officer, Major Benton, in July 1915.
Counsel: What sort of revolver was it?
Light: A Webley & Scott service revolver.
Counsel: What became of it?
Light: When I was injured in August 1918, it was taken away from me with all my other kit.
Counsel: Have you ever seen that revolver since that time?
Light: Never.
Counsel: Did the revolver come with a holster?
Light: Yes.
Counsel: Did you take this to France with you?
Light: Only on the first occasion – when I was with the Royal Engineers. I did not take it on the second.

Benton confirmed to the police that he had sold a Webley & Scott service revolver, but could not remember to whom. When Light commenced duty with the Honourable Artillery Company in November 1917, he had taken this revolver to France but not the holster because privates were not permitted to wear them (it appears he had kept his weapon in his backpack). There was no independent confirmation that Light's weapon had been confiscated. If Light's testimony is to be believed, he owned a holster but no revolver at the time of Bella Wright's death.

Marshall Hall's next task was to guide his client through the events of Saturday 5 July 1919.

Counsel: At what time did you leave your house?
Light: Around half-past five.
Counsel: How were you dressed?
Light: I was wearing an old suit.
Counsel: I will ask this just once: was there any pocket in that suit in which you could have carried a service revolver?
Light: Certainly not.
Counsel: Had you in your possession at that time any revolver?
Light: No.
Counsel: Have you at any time possessed any revolver other than the one you bought from your commanding officer?
Light: No.
Counsel: Had you any ammunition?
Light: Yes.
Counsel: And were they .455 calibre for the service revolver?
Light: Yes.
Counsel (referring to the bullets retrieved from the canal): Are these cartridges yours?
Light: As far as I know.

Chapter 6

Light denied possessing the service revolver but not the holster and ammunition that were fished out of the canal. Marshall Hall continued to ask questions about his movements on the day Bella Wright died.

Counsel: On that Saturday, did you see a young lady riding a bicycle?

Light: Yes.

Counsel: Which way was she riding?

Light: As a matter of fact, when I first saw her she was standing by her bicycle at the roadside.

Counsel: What was she doing?

Light: She was bending over it.

Counsel: Had you ever seen her before?

Light: Never.

Counsel: In your own words, what happened next?

Light: As I came up to the young lady she was stooping over her bicycle. As I approached, she looked up and asked me if I had a spanner. I had no spanners with me, but I looked at her bicycle. As far as I could see, there was a certain amount of play in the freewheel, but without any spanners I could do nothing. I then rode on with the girl.

Counsel: Where did you eventually arrive?

Light: We came to a village. I asked her the name of it, and she said it was called Gaulby.

Counsel: Did she say anything else?

Light: Yes, as we got there she told me she was visiting friends and said, "I shall only be 10 minutes or a quarter of an hour." I accompanied her as far as the house where she was going.

Counsel: Was anything said about you waiting?

Light: Well, not in so many words.

Counsel: Would you explain that?

Light: When she said, "I shall only be 10 minutes or a quarter of an hour," I took that as a sort of suggestion that I should wait and that we should ride together.

Counsel: For how long did you wait?

Light: I waited in the lane for about a quarter of an hour.

Counsel: What did you do next?

Light: I walked my machine up the hill to the church then I got on it, intending to go straight to Leicester, but found my back tyre was flat. I got off my machine and pumped it up, but it went flat again and I had to mend it with my repair kit.

Counsel: At what time did you finish mending your tyre?

Light: About quarter past eight. I knew it was late, but I thought I would see where the girl had got to.

Counsel: Did you ride back to the house?

Light: Yes. I saw her coming out of the house.

Counsel: Were you riding your bicycle?

Light: Yes, down the hill from the church, but before I got to the cottage I dismounted and walked to the gate.

Counsel: Did you speak to the girl?

Light: Yes, I said, "Hello, you've been a long time. I thought you had gone the other way."

Counsel: Did you call her Bella?

Light: No.

Counsel: Did you know her name?

Light: No.

Counsel: Did you have a conversation with the witness, Evans?

Light: Yes.

Counsel: Apart from you not saying "Bella", is his evidence fairly accurate?

Light: Yes.

Counsel: Did you leave with the girl?

Light: Yes.

Counsel: When did you get on your bicycles?

Light: At the top of the hill, by the church.

Counsel: What happened next?

Light: My tyre started to go flat. I had to pump it up again. The girl rode ahead very slowly.

Counsel: Did you ride after her?

Light: Yes, she was about a couple of hundred yards ahead.

According to Light, he and Bella soon parted company at a junction in the road. Bearing right, it headed west towards Leicester, but turning off to the left, passing through a gate, it headed south {see *Exhibit C which shows the place where the two separated according to Light*}.

Counsel: When you reached the junction, was there any conversation?

Light: Yes, as I turned right she got off her bicycle, saying, "I must say goodbye to you here. I am going that way," and pointed to the road on the left of the gate. I pointed to the road I was on and said: "But isn't this the way to Leicester?" She said, "I don't live there." I said, "Well, I must go this way because I am late already and with this puncture I may have to walk home."

Counsel: When would this be?

Light: About 10 minutes after leaving Gaulby.

Counsel: After parting company, did you ever see her again?

Light: No.

Counsel: How long did it take you to get home?

Light: Some time. I had to pump up my tyre several times. It kept going down every five minutes or so.

Counsel: Eventually, what did you do?

Light: It got so bad that I had to walk and got home just before 10 o'clock.

The prosecution counsel, Henry Maddocks, cross-examined Light on some of these points. The following is an abridged account of the exchanges between them.

Counsel: Before arriving at Gaulby, did you know where the deceased was heading?

Light: No.

Counsel: Or where she lived?

Light: No.

Counsel: For all you knew, she might have lived to the east of Gaulby?

Light: She might have done.

Counsel: As you had to head west to return to Leicester, it was futile to wait for her?

Light: But for the fact that she told me she would only be a few minutes. And I assumed she would probably be going back the way she came.

Counsel: Were you so interested in the girl that you would wait and see her when she came out of the house, for the purpose of accompanying her home?

Light: I was not.

Light's answers, even under cross-examination, were plausible. He thought Bella wanted him to wait and did so for 15 minutes. Tired of waiting, he decided to leave, but was delayed by about an hour to repair a puncture. He then thought he might as well see if Bella was leaving, thinking she would be heading back the way she had come. If you are more sceptical, you might think that by stonewalling after his arrest, there had been plenty of time for Light to concoct a credible story.

The prosecution also questioned Light about his journey home:

Counsel: At what time did you part from Bella?
Light: When I left her at the gate road it would be about 8:40pm.
Counsel: I understand, then, that it took you 1 hour 20 minutes to get home?
Light: It took me about 1 hour 10 minutes to get home, arriving before 10.
Counsel: During your journey home did you meet anybody?
Light: After I came to Evington I met a great deal of people.
Counsel: Did you cycle through Stoughton?
Light: Yes, but I walked the greater part of the way after Evington.

Light says he met a great deal of people after Evington, yet none came forward when the police appealed for information. This point appears to have been missed by the prosecution, but you should bear it in mind — we will examine Light's journey home later.

We have heard Light's version of events on the fatal evening. Not surprisingly, the story he tells is that he was innocently caught up in the tragedy. This leads to perhaps the most important issue of all. If this were true, why had Light behaved as though he was guilty after the event? The following is an abridged account of the exchanges between Light and the prosecution counsel, Henry Maddocks, on this very point:

Counsel: With regard to the recovered holster and cycle parts, there has never been the slightest doubt they belonged to you?

Light: Never the slightest doubt.

Counsel: Did you throw all the bicycle parts in on one occasion?

Light: Yes, all on one night.

Counsel: Did you file off the number from the bicycle frame?

Light: Yes.

Counsel: At home?

Light: Yes.

Counsel: When?

Light: Shortly before I decided to throw the machine away.

Counsel: When would this have been?

Light: It was shortly after summertime had finished, that's all I can recollect. That would be October.

Counsel: Why did you do this?

Light: In view of the case, I wanted to get rid of the machine.

Counsel: Why did you file off the identification number from the bicycle?

Light: I did not want the bicycle traced to me.

Counsel: Feeling secure, is that why you denied owning a green bicycle to Superintendent Taylor?

Chapter 6

Light: I said the very first thing that came into my head.

Counsel: Why did you tell the police you had sold the green bicycle?

Light: Well, I had drifted into this policy of concealing the fact that I had been out riding that night and had to go on with it.

Counsel: On the Saturday night, did you carry a raincoat?

Light: Yes, over my shoulder.

Counsel: What happened to it?

Light: I sold it.

Counsel: Why?

Light: It was old.

Counsel (sarcastically): Did you sell your trousers, too? *(Laughter in court)*

Light: I cannot remember.

Counsel: Did you see the police notices asking for information regarding the man with the green bicycle?

Light: I saw what was in the newspapers, but not the handbills.

Counsel: But you knew the police were anxious to find the man with the green bicycle?

Light: Yes.

Counsel: Why not say it was you?

Light: Because I was absolutely dazed about the whole thing, and I did not think clearly about it, and could not make up my mind what to do.

Counsel (holding up a clipping from the *Leicester Mercury*): When you read this account, was it the first time you had heard about the death of the girl you had cycled with?

Light: Yes.

Counsel: And this was the first time you knew she was called Bella Wright?

Light: Yes.

Counsel: Why could you have not given the police an explanation that you were the man on the green bicycle?

Light: Because everyone had apparently jumped to the conclusion that the man with the green bicycle had murdered the girl.

Judge (intervening): You said that you could not have been of any assistance by going to the police. Do you not see that you could have greatly helped the police?

Light: I see it now, of course. I did not deliberately make up my mind not to go forward. I was astounded and frightened at this unexpected thing. I kept on hesitating, and in the end drifted into doing nothing at all.

Judge: But you could have told the police, "Come and search my house. You will see I have no revolver."

Light: I could not think clearly of those things then, my Lord.

Judge: Finding yourself in this situation, innocent and having nothing to do with it, did you go to your mother for advice on what to do?

Light: No. One of the chief reasons why I did not come forward was that I did not want to worry my mother.

Counsel (resuming cross-examination): Was it because you feared no one would believe your story and that it pointed to you having had something to do with her death?

Light: No, I did not think that.

Judge (intervening): In which case, it seems even more extraordinary that you did not tell people.

Light: I did not realise what a difficult position I was putting myself in.

Judge: You were not prepared to give information about the discovery of a very serious crime?

Light: I could give no information whatsoever, my Lord, as to the cause of her death.

Judge: But don't you see, you could have provided useful information to the police?

Light: I see it now, my Lord.

Counsel (resuming cross-examination): When the housekeeper, Mary Webb, mentioned the murder to you, why did you not say that you had been the man on the green bicycle?

Light: I had not made up my mind whether to come forward or not at that time. If I had told anybody, I would have had to come forward and tell everybody.

Innocent or guilty, Ronald Light had thought extremely carefully about his testimony. Compare the words he used in his cross-examination with those in his written brief to Marshall Hall. They are remarkably similar. Indeed, the only point absent from the written instruction was the reference to his mother, and one wonders if Light would have mentioned his mother at all had he not been asked about her.

Members of the Cold Case Jury, you have now read Ronald Light's testimony on the most important aspects of the case. Not surprisingly, the prosecution was less than impressed with his answers. In his closing speech, Henry Maddocks asked the jury how it could reasonably accept anything that Light had said after his silence. The prisoner had taken all possible steps a guilty man could have taken to cover up his crime. Not only had Light kept silent but, given the first opportunity to explain himself, he had lied. His only course of action was to hope that no further evidence connected him to the case beyond his alleged parting with Bella Wright.

To remind the jury of this last point was unwise. As Edward Marjoribanks points out in *Famous Trials of Marshall Hall* (1950), the prosecution failed entirely to place Light by the victim's side at the moment of her death.

When the cover-up failed, Maddocks continued, Light took the only other course available to him – to say that he knew nothing and that he was so dazed he did not know what to do. Why was he so dazed? It could only have been for one reason: that his explanation would not be believed.

Marshall Hall, in his closing speech, stressed the absence of motive. Had the jury members any doubt in their minds that the dead girl was telling the truth when she said the man was "a perfect stranger"? There was no evidence that the girl had been assaulted, no sign of a struggle. Was it to be believed that this man, having been merely rebuffed by a woman he did not know, shot her in cold blood? Such a man would have done what he wanted first, then shot her, Marshall Hall claimed. Also, where had the accused concealed the weapon? The descriptions of the man and his bicycle were accurate to the last detail – would not the witnesses have also noticed something heavy in his raincoat pocket, such as a service revolver? Yet not a single word was said about it.

Marshall Hall conceded that his client had shown moral

cowardice of the worst possible order in not coming forward, but the jury should consider that he had suffered shellshock from the war, and also did not want to alarm his mother.

Marshall Hall also submitted to the jury that his client's behaviour was borne of fear rather than a will to deceive. Anyone could see there was a ready-made story that he could have told: the young woman had been killed accidentally. Perhaps they had been looking at the revolver when it went off by itself. "There's not a man, woman or child who would not have accepted that story. There was the man's perfect defence if he wanted to invent a defence... it's practically examination-proof. But it was not his story."

After the judge's summing up, the jury went away to consider its verdict. Wakefield, who discussed the case with one of the jurors when writing his book, says the jury was deadlocked. Three of the 12 were doggedly holding out for a guilty verdict. After an absence of three hours, the judge recalled the jurors, asking them if there was any chance of agreement on the verdict. The foreman believed there was, and requested a little more time, which was granted. The judge's intervention obviously had an impact. Three minutes later the jury returned, the dissenters having thrown in the towel. The verdict was 'not guilty'.

Ronald Vivian Light had escaped the hangman's noose. Within days of his acquittal, he wrote to Marshall Hall thanking him for saving his life: "I shall always remember you with the greatest gratitude." As well as he might, because he had been stuck in evidential quicksand – the more he denied, the more he sank. It had been a desperate fight to pull him free. Little wonder Marshall Hall thought it was his "greatest success as an advocate".

Despite the verdict, it had also been a success for Leicestershire Constabulary. The Assistant Principal for the Director of Public Prosecutions wrote to Edward Holmes, the Chief Constable, expressing his gratitude for the "extremely able manner in which the police investigation was carried out", which was "marked by a sense of fairness and a degree of intelligence" that was appreciated by both the judge and the prosecution team.

But questions remained. Had Light's reticence to tell the truth almost put him on the gallows, or had he got away with murder? Following Light's acquittal, armchair detectives poured over "one of the most outstanding and absorbing murder puzzles of all time". In particular, one aspect of the case was intriguing. Although ignored during the trial, was the dead crow in the cornfield the key to solving the case?

Chapter 7

SHOOTING CROWS

D espite his earlier denials, Ronald Light was the man on the green bicycle. He was traced by police, tried for the murder of Bella Wright and acquitted. The jury harboured a reasonable doubt about his guilt, probably because Marshall Hall had disputed the ballistics evidence and left open the possibility that Bella was shot by someone else, although he did not advance any alternative theory of how Bella might have died. As the defence barrister, he needed only to show that the prosecution's case against his client was not legally sufficient for the jury to convict. However, others have speculated on what might have occurred on that July evening.

Less than two years after the trial, in February 1922, writer Trueman Humphries developed the 'shooting crows' theory in an article for *The Strand Magazine*. Although it was a fictional account, inspired by the Sherlock Holmes stories, the author had taken photographs of the crime scene and assiduously gathered the known facts. This is how the magazine introduced the article:

Here is something new! Every reader will remember the dramatic Green Bicycle Case. Ronald Light was found innocent, but the mystery remains – who shot Bella Wright? The writer of this story, after a most careful investigation, here puts forward, in the novel form of mingled fact and fiction, his theory of what actually occurred.

The following reconstruction is built upon the factual foundations of this theory. It assumes that Light was never involved in Bella's death and that he told the truth, albeit belatedly. He was in the wrong place at the wrong time riding a distinctive bicycle. He was not a murderer, guilty only of moral cowardice in not coming forward to explain everything to the police.

I have ignored Humphries' overblown fictional elements, but my account does include some speculative narrative. For example, Light claimed to have suffered shellshock (a type of fear conditioned in combat, typically with flash-backs), which, he told the court, had "upset his nervous system" and he had not been the same since. We do not know what he experienced during his time in France, or how seriously it affected him, so I have taken dramatic licence in attributing to him certain war experiences. Nevertheless, the described experiences are not conjecture; they are genuine first-hand accounts of World War I veterans (see Part Three for the sources).

Let us return to rural Leicestershire at 6:45pm on Saturday 5 July 1919. Bella Wright has less than three hours to live.

Chapter 7

Ronald Light cycled leisurely up the small hill. Not far from the top the hedgerows were festooned with bouquets of white and yellow flowers, or so it appeared. As he approached, the flowers took flight as hundreds of cabbage white and brimstone butterflies fluttered into the air. For a moment the sky was filled with shimmering colour, as if confetti had been thrown into the wind. Light stopped. Memories surged into his consciousness like breaking waves.

"They're souls, every one of them," said the sergeant, planting his rifle by his side. "Human souls," he emphasised, "on their final flight to the afterlife."

Gunner Light followed his sergeant's gaze. Several hundred yards away on the side of an incline was a small copse, an oasis in a desert of mud, craters, twisted tree stumps and barbed wire. From the daubs of greenery a profusion of yellow and white fluttered into the air.

"I think they're butterflies, sir."

"I know what they are, Private," his superior replied firmly, his gaze held by the unfolding spectacle. "The spirits of the fallen are being carried away from this hell on the wings of butterflies. Look at them go!"

Light was unsure what to say. "It's a beautiful thought," he finally remarked.

"If I go, I want to fly out of here like that. Can you imagine it, Light? To slip your mortal chains and be carried away on the wing. If you see a butterfly when you get back to Blighty, it will be one of the lads returning home. Remember that. God's speed, lads!"

Worried that his sergeant was about to drop his rifle and

walk across the fields of mud to a certain death, Light touched his comrade's shoulder. It broke the trance into which he had fallen.

Light took a cigarette from the inside of his jacket and placed it between his lips. He remained there, smoking, transfixed by the butterflies as they fluttered over the lane and swirled around his bicycle until the last brimstone flitted over a blackthorn bush and into an adjoining field. "It's a beautiful thought," he said to himself, flicking his unfinished cigarette onto the road. He remounted his bicycle and soon crested the hill.

A few yards further, at a T-junction, a woman dressed in a pastel blouse and long skirt was hunched over a bicycle propped against a fingerboard signpost. Light slowed. "Anything the matter?" he called out.

On hearing the high-pitched voice behind her, Bella straightened up and turned, steadying her wide-brimmed straw hat in the breeze. "You gave me a start! I never heard you coming."

"Is everything alright? It looks like you are having a spot of bother."

"You don't have a spanner, do you?"

Light stopped opposite the woman. "No, I don't. What seems to be the problem?"

"Oh, the freewheel is loose. I'm sure it just needs tightening." Light found the woman's voice sweet and soft. It sounded alluringly diffident, almost vulnerable.

"Let me have a look." He dismounted, leaning his bicycle against a hedge. He removed his raincoat, which was draped over his right shoulder, placing it over the handlebars of his bike. He took hold of the woman's bicycle, wheeling it into the road. "May I?"

Bella nodded as Light mounted it. He peddled slowly, cycling several yards along the lane before returning. "You're right, it does need tightening." Light dismounted and fiddled with the wheel. After a while he presented the bicycle to Bella. "That's the best I can do without a spanner. Where are you headed?"

She pointed down the road, heading east. "This way."

"I'm going that way myself. Do you mind if I accompany you?"

Bella hesitated. She was a little uncomfortable cycling with an older man, especially one who could not be bothered to shave. Her mother had told her that such men had a lack of respect and should not be trusted. On the other hand, he had tried to help her. "Alright, but I'm not interesting company, I'm afraid." They mounted their machines and cycled eastwards.

7:15pm. The conversation had been a little one-sided. Bella was circumspect, preferring not to give away too much information about herself, especially to people she did not know well. By contrast, Light was loquacious, even if his shrill voice grated after a while.

"So you served in France?" Bella queried.

"Yes, at the Somme with the Royal Engineers, and with the Honourable Artillery Company."

"Were you sent over the top?"

"No, I was constructing trenches, and then I was a gunner. I'm still slightly deaf from the noise of the constant shelling. The sound of our guns was worse than the enemy's!

Sometimes the bombardments lasted for days. You couldn't escape the noise or the shaking ground, night or day. Some of the lads were driven crazy by it."

"It sounds awful."

"Well, the gunfire was not the worst thing. Ask any veteran what he hated most, and I bet the answer will be the same." He paused for dramatic effect. "The lice."

"Lice?" Bella was surprised and repulsed in equal measure.

"The blighters would get into your clothing. If you did not get rid of them you would be covered in a rash of angry bites. The itch was unbearable."

"Couldn't you wash them out?"

Light laughed. "The army tried everything, even steam-cleaning our uniforms. Nothing worked. The only way to delouse was to run a lighted candle down the seam to burn them out, one by one. It was the same every night: men huddled over a candle, holding a crummy jacket or pair of trousers."

"That's a strange word – crummy."

"Oh, the blasted eggs looked like breadcrumbs. You had to get rid of the eggs or you would be infested within days. I remember one lad had such a crummy shirt that he wrote home asking his mother to send over some insect powder. A week later a package arrived with his usual letter. Sure enough, his mother had sent him some Keating's powder. We were all envious that night, as he rubbed his chest and back with the stuff when he turned in. He awoke in agony hours later, though. They had crawled to his neck! It was so raw it looked like he was wearing a red neckerchief. It got infected after a day or two and he went to the infirmary. I don't know what happened to him. I suspect it was a Blighty One."

Light noticed his young companion was puzzled at his last comment. "That's an injury that wasn't too serious but got you sent back home. All the lads prayed for it, even the atheists! Mind you, it was back to the Front as soon as you had recovered."

The cyclists passed a farmer tending to his cattle in a neighbouring field. They did not notice him, but Thomas Nourish would later testify that he saw a young woman and an older, unshaven man cycling towards Gaulby sometime after 7pm on Saturday 5 July.

7:25pm. "That's a grand-looking church," Light remarked. "What's this village?"

"Gaulby. My uncle lives here."

The couple cycled by St Peter's church, with its ornate pinnacles rising from each corner of the tower, and a parked carriers' van before turning right and down a hill, passing a line of semi-detached houses. Bella slowed. "There's my uncle's cottage," she said, gesturing to a red-brick house a dozen yards away. "I shall only be 10 minutes or quarter of an hour."

Light took the hint: the young woman wanted him to wait. Why else would she bother telling him that she would only be inside for such a short time? Needing no further encouragement, he pulled his bicycle to the far side of the road by an elderberry bush. Moments later he observed the carriers' van stopping outside the cottage that Bella had entered. A man with a full-flowing beard answered the knock at the door.

8pm. Light had no need to check his pocket watch to know that the girl had been far longer than 10 minutes. On seeing the old bearded man appear at the cottage window like a grumpy troll, he decided wisely to cycle on. He freewheeled to the bottom of the lane and turned into Back Lane, which led to St Peter's church and the Leicester road. He was approaching the church when his rear tyre flattened. The slow puncture, caused by deterioration of the rubber in the inner tube, had been a persistent problem. He pulled over to a fingerpost. Pumping up the tyre was hopeless – as soon as he stopped, it deflated. He took out the repair kit from his saddle bag and started a temporary fix.

8:35pm. The repair took longer than Light had anticipated. He knew he was already late for dinner, so there was no harm in looking for the girl, although he expected that she had left the cottage long ago. As Light started the gentle descent from the church, he saw a group of people talking outside the cottage. As he approached, he saw the young woman was leaving. "Hello," he said to her breezily, "you have been a long time. I thought you had gone the other way." Bella looked uncomfortable.

"That's an unusual colour," Jim Evans remarked, pointing at Light's bicycle.

"Pea green," replied Light in his high-pitch squeal. "It's a BSA, deluxe."

"I've got a BSA too. May I take a look?"

"Be my guest. It's a heavy machine." While Bella talked to her relatives, Light was happy to discuss his bicycle's features.

8:45pm. "Well, I'd better be going," Bella announced. After saying her farewells to her relatives, she started pushing her bicycle up the gentle incline toward the church. Light turned his bicycle around and walked beside her.

"Why did you wait?" Bella asked.

"I had a puncture. It took me the best part of an hour to fix it."

"You suddenly got a puncture, did you?" she queried mockingly.

"The rear tyre's in a bad way. It's so porous. I should have replaced it ages ago, but you know how expensive they are these days."

"I can get them at cost price, you know. That's one advantage of working at a tyre factory!" Light was about to ask Bella whether she would be able to obtain one on his behalf when she changed the subject. "Do you think it is going to rain? I hope not. I hate cycling in the wet."

He looked skywards. "If anything, the weather looks brighter to the west, but I came prepared." He pointed to his mackintosh. "Some summer, eh?"

Bella stopped and put on her light raincoat. They cycled away from Gaulby church and along the Leicester road. **9pm.** After passing the turning to King's Norton they were serenaded by the most beautiful warbling. "Oh, I love nightingales," Bella enthused. "I could listen to their song all day. It's like… I don't know… an aria," she giggled. "You know what I mean?"

"Yeah." He recognised the birdsong instantly. He had heard it at the Somme, of all places. One dawn, a nightingale perched in a nearby copse and had started to sing, its intricate melody soaring above the incessant, deafening noise of the shelling. Everyone in the trench had stopped and listened. It was magical: a small bird defying the pounding guns!

Bella pulled over to her left and stopped by a rickety gate. "I must say goodbye to you here," she said.

Light frowned: "Here?"

"I'm taking this road."

Pointing to the road ahead, he declared: "But this is the quickest way to Leicester!"

"But I don't live there," Bella replied, opening the gate. She walked her bicycle through, closing it before Light could follow. She did not want to risk being seen near Stoughton in the company of a strange man and start the inevitable gossiping. She thought it best to separate for the rest of the journey home. It was a fateful decision.

Light's voice was dampened by disappointment: "Well, I must go this way. I'm late already. And with this puncture, who knows? I may have to walk home!"

As he watched the young woman cycle along the lane, he called out after her: "I don't know your name!" Bella heard but kept cycling.

9:10pm. The sound of gunfire sent a scattering of birds into the air. "Damn!" exclaimed the solitary youth wearing an army jacket and heavy boots. It was the second time he had missed his target – a crow perched high in a beech tree. He was not a good shot. In fact, it was the first time he had handled a rifle, let alone fired one. The youth had pestered his older brother on numerous occasions to take him shooting, but he had always been turned down, the rifle staying securely locked away in a trunk at the end of his bed. The previous week, the youth had discovered the hiding

Chapter 7

place of the key in his brother's bedroom: it was kept behind a novel on the bookshelf. Then it was a matter of waiting until his brother next stayed overnight with his friend in Market Harborough for the youth to seize his opportunity. And the rifle.

The joy shooter skirted by the edge of the cornfield until he reached a stile. The adjacent field was a meadow of shin-high grass with a sheep trough near its centre. Spurred on by the thought of shooting a rabbit, the youth clambered over. It was not long before he saw several white tails bobbing up and down. He lay down by the metal trough and rested his gun on one of its sides to steady his aim. The dark clouds in the west parted, allowing the sinking sun to bathe the meadow in a golden glow. He noticed a crow land on top of a field gate some 25 yards away, a little to his right. The gate, situated on the northern boundary of the meadow, flanked by high hedgerows, provided entry to and from the Via Devana road, was the only gap: the rest of the road was invisible to anyone in the meadow. Having missed two crows already, the youth set his sights on settling unfinished business. He carefully lined up the stationary bird in his sights. His finger tightened around the trigger.

As Bella neared the field gate, the crow squawked. She glanced to her left. The shooter pulled the trigger.

In an instant, the bullet entered the left side of the crow, exited, and continued its trajectory. Bella died instantly, the bullet's force pushing her head back, creating sufficient momentum for her to fall backwards onto the road, her legs sprawled on the verge. Her bicycle crashed to the ground, its wheel pointing in the direction of travel towards Leicester.

The shooter only saw his quarry flap its wings, lurch forward and fall from the gate. He was surprised to hear the screeching of metal from beyond the hedgerow. He stood up. To his great annoyance, the fatally injured crow flapped back to the top of the gate, where it remained for a few moments, before flying laboriously over the meadow in the direction of the cornfield behind the hapless hunter.

Curious, the youth walked to the gate. He stepped on its bottom rung and bent over the top, peering to his right. Lying next to a bicycle was a woman prostrate on the road, blood oozing from her head. He felt sick and started to shake. He was sure the woman was dead and he dared not risk being seen in the road hunched over the still body. He was responsible, after all.

From a nearby field he heard a cow bellow. In panic, he turned and fled across the meadow towards the cornfield, retracing his steps in the tracks he had left earlier. He soon reached the stile, bounded over it in one leap and raced home. Once inside the cottage, he walked to his brother's bedroom, locked away the rifle and placed the key exactly where he had found it: behind *The Man Who Knew* by Edgar Wallace.

Members of the Cold Case Jury, when Trueman Humphries visited Stretton Parva he made copious notes and took several photographs of the scene where Bella had died. He found the height of the meadow gate to be 4'2" and the distance from the gate to the road approximately three yards. In the grassy meadow he discovered a sheep trough, some 25 yards from the gate, and offset to its right when looking from the road.

In his account, Humphries suggests that a shooter, lying on the ground, used the trough to steady his aim. From this position, a bullet fired in an upwards trajectory hit the crow sitting on the gate, and continued upwards to hit Bella in the head {see *Exhibit D*}. He believes the bullet travelled a further six yards down the road, where it landed, spent. Later, it was trodden upon by passing traffic and then famously discovered by PC Alfred Hall. It all seems to fit, but does it hold together under closer examination?

First, could a bullet fired from the sheep trough in the field have hit Bella in the head? Yes, basic trigonometry shows us that when the bullet reached the road it could have been at approximately head height (about 5ft from the ground). However, in this calculation we have to make many assumptions, including that the ground between the trough and the road was level. In fact, there are far too many variables to calculate this answer with any confidence. Therefore, we cannot say for certain the bullet would have hit Bella Wright where it did. We can say only that it is possible Bella Wright was shot in the way Humphries suggests.

Second, is there any evidence that the dead crow was shot? Elizabeth Villiers, in her article *The Mystery of the Green Bicycle* (1928), castigates PC Hall for not having the crow examined by an expert immediately after it was found in the cornfield. This criticism is unwarranted: it was examined, although not by an expert. We know this from the report made by Detective Chief Inspector Hawkins, one of the Scotland Yard officers {see *Exhibit 6*}. Referring to the blood-stains found on the top of the gate, he writes:

Shooting Crows

An examination by Superintendent Taylor was made on July 7 and he was satisfied they had been caused by a bird which had been standing in the pool of blood by the deceased, of which it had gorged itself, then hopped about on the gate, and then flew across the field of mowing grass and fell dead in an adjacent field of corn. The bird's feet (a crow) were covered in congealed blood. It was opened by Taylor with the idea of seeing if it had been shot but the conclusion was that the bird, whose crop was full of new blood, had died by choking. Certainly there was no trace of a bullet, or of a bullet or shot wound.

The police believed that the crow had died from gorging on blood. This supposition is not without its problems, however, as neatly phrased by Edmund Pearson in *The Death of Bella Wright* (1964):

How did the bird obtain so much blood from the poor dead or dying girl to cause its own death? Since the body is supposed to have been found within minutes of death, how was there time for all this gruesome feasting and tracking back and forth from road to gate?

To which it may be added: and was this a new species of crow, *Corvus dracula*? Although a carrion crow or a rook would be attracted to a dead body, not least because they are curious animals, humans are an unfamiliar food source. It would most likely take a few days for a bird to attempt feeding. The body of Bella Wright was found less than half an hour after she was shot. So, Pearson's suggestion that a blood-gorging crow would have fed swiftly can also be questioned. If the crow consumed the blood from the road after the body had been moved, there was no need for it to binge feed.

Even if the blood-gorging crow supposition is accepted, rather than the idea that the crow was shot dead, the 'shooting crows' theory should not be rejected too hastily. It is possible that the shooter missed the perched crow, but hit Bella, and then the blood-drinking crow helped itself to a late meal. The problem with this amended theory is that there is no independent evidence there was ever anyone shooting crows: it is only from a shot crow that we infer there was a crow shooter. Perhaps this can be countered by pointing out there is evidence that someone at some time had been shooting in this area: the spent bullet on the road. However, it is a .455 calibre bullet, and we are back to the dispute over ballistics.

So, is the 'shooting crows' theory consistent with the ballistics evidence? Humphries assumes that Bella was shot by a .455 calibre rifle and the bullet was subsequently found on the road by Constable Hall. Russell Wakefield in *The Green Bicycle Case* argues this is unlikely:

Bella Wright died from a .455 calibre bullet passing through her head, and bullets of that calibre are either fired from a revolver or an elephant rifle. It is a severe strain on one's credibility to suggest that there are many sportsmen easing off elephant rifles across Leicestershire lanes.

Further, as its name suggests, an elephant rifle is a powerful weapon capable of bringing down big game. Even if the target was 25 yards away, it is likely to inflict far more serious injuries than Bella sustained. Certainly, the crow would have been blown apart had it been hit. The 'shooting crows' theory appears untenable, if the shooter used a large calibre rifle as Humphries supposed.

The theory can be saved, however, if we assume that the shooter used a smaller calibre rifle – and the reconstruction intentionally did not specify the calibre of the rifle. A .30 rook rifle would be a good candidate, for instance. It is a smaller calibre firearm that might be found in a farming community and, as its name suggests, it is used to kill crows. If this amended theory is accepted then the .455 bullet found in the road was unconnected to the case; you have to believe that it being found near the dead body was a pure coincidence.

But is this amended theory consistent with the medical evidence? In particular, what is the significance of the tiny metal fragments found by Dr Williams by the entrance wound in Bella's cheek? If it is stippling (a pattern of gunpowder or metal fragments discharged from a gun muzzle), this implies the shooter fired his weapon from not more than two yards away. It should be noted, however, that there is no mention of stippling in the autopsy report {see *Exhibit 3*}. Dr Williams told the police in a statement:

I cannot believe that the bullet was fired from a long distance as I would suppose the small pieces of metal found in the entrance wound to be absent. Also, the wounds of entrance and exit would be quite different in character.

Clearly, such a view is inconsistent with any version of the 'shooting crows' theory. Wendy East writes:

Is it even remotely possible that she was shot by someone out rooking whom the police failed to trace? The answer is clear. The bullet that killed Bella Wright was fired from a distance of probably no more than six feet.

East is correct to couch her conclusion in terms of

probability, as any ballistics expert will say that, to have a high degree of confidence in any assessment, the actual murder weapon must be test fired to understand its unique idiosyncrasies. Despite the ballistic evidence, the 'shooting crows' theory has been popular with crime writers. Elizabeth Villiers writes, "the more this theory is examined, the more it seems to be convincing". John Rowland concurs, in *The Green Bicycle Case* (1963), stating, "this theory seems to have the best basis". Other writers have dissented from this view, believing that Ronald Light got away with murder. It is to this theory we now turn.

Chapter 8

A DIFFERENT LIGHT

In the previous reconstruction, Ronald Light was portrayed sympathetically. However, we know for sure that he exhibited at least one of the three 'dark personality' attributes: manipulation. Light's forging of the War Office telegram is an extraordinary example. He appears to have had another: narcissism, a bloated sense of self-importance and entitlement. His doting mother might have unwittingly fostered such an attitude. Completing the 'dark triad' is psychopathy, a dangerous impulsiveness combined with extremely low empathy. The following reconstruction assumes that Light possessed all three, giving him a personality type often seen in murderers.

This reconstruction does not accept Ronald Light's trial testimony and presumes that he murdered Bella Wright. In particular, it assumes that he knew Bella Wright and was prone to making sexual advances – the evidence for which will be discussed later. To see how and why Light might have been led to murder, let us again rewind time to

Chapter 8

Saturday 5 July 1919.

6pm. Schoolgirls Muriel Nunney and Valeria Caven were enjoying a cycle ride in the countryside. Muriel was 14 years old, with bobbed wavy hair. Impish-looking Valeria was two years her junior. The close friends were cycling on the Via Devana, a mile or so from the outskirts of Leicester. This part of the lane, lined with hedgerows punctuated by beautiful copper beeches, cut through mixed farmland.

"What's that bird, Val?" Muriel pointed to a thrush-like bird with a finch's beak. "It don't half have a loud song!"

"Looks like a corn buntin'," her slight friend replied, straining her neck to see it at the top of a small tree. "I think so, anyway."

In the distance a cyclist was approaching. As he drew closer, the girls noticed it was a man riding a green bicycle. They both observed he was unshaven and wearing a light suit, a raincoat draped over one shoulder. He slowed and looked across at the girls, before drifting slowly past.

"Did you see the way that man looked at us?" Val asked her friend.

"Not really."

"It was funny."

"Well, he needs a shave. Ma says it makes a man look unclean if he don't."

"No, the way he stared... it was dead creepy."

The girls continued at their leisurely pace, amused by a bouquet of pheasants darting in and out of the hedgerows. Val heard a noise from behind and looked over her shoulder. "He's following us!" she whispered urgently, her eyes wide with surprise.

Muriel looked back and saw the man on the green bicycle following a dozen or so yards behind. "He'll be gone soon, I expect." They continued cycling for several minutes, each looking over their shoulder every so often. Each time they looked, the man was still behind them, and they became ever more worried by his presence.

"I don't like this," Val said to her friend.

"Me neither."

They cycled down a gentle hill, at the bottom of which was an isolated farmhouse. "Let's stop here," Muriel said. Both girls dismounted. Nervously, they watched as the man drew beside them and stopped.

"Hey, girls, what are you doing?" Light asked, in his squeaky voice. Val sniggered, and received an elbow in her side for her rudeness.

"Nothing!" replied Muriel.

"You're not doing nothing, I can see that much!" The girls looked blankly at him. "Where are you going?" Val was about to answer, but her older friend glowered at her.

"Cat's got your tongues, I see. Why don't we have some fun? I know a game we could play."

"What game?" Val asked.

"Val!" implored Muriel, angrily placing a finger to her lips.

"Follow the leader. You stay here," he said pointing at Valeria. He then looked at Muriel, "You cycle on with me." Too anxious to speak, Muriel shook her head.

"Alright, you stay." Light pointed at Valeria a second time. "*You* be the leader. Come on." Light pushed off.

"No. We're going home now," Muriel said, as assertively

as she could. "Come on, Val." The girls turned their bicycles around and cycled back up the hill without looking behind. As soon as they crested the top they pedalled as hard as they possibly could until they were certain the man was no longer following.

Light pulled his bicycle over to the side of the road to pump up his rear tyre, having felt it was a little flat. After a smoke, he decided to carry on cycling away from Leicester. Fifteen minutes later he turned and headed north towards the Leicester road, which he knew ran parallel to the Via Devana.

6:45pm. Ronald Light saw the young woman by the side of the road, bent over her bicycle. As he drew nearer he recognised her. "Bella!" he called out excitedly.

Bella's heart sank like a dropped anchor. The shrill voice was unmistakable. She straightened up and was a little shocked to see the pest was unshaven and unkempt. "Oh," she replied unenthusiastically. On several occasions over the past few months, Light had been waiting for Bella in Shady Lane as she returned home from the mill. They had spoken. She had told him she was soon to be married, but it did not deter him.

"You can't say I've been hanging around for you today," he squeaked, dismounting his bicycle. "What's the problem?"

She held her wide-brimmed straw hat as it flapped in the breeze. "There's something wrong with the freewheel, I think."

"Let me take a look." He dismounted, leaning his bicycle against a hedge. When he placed his raincoat over the handlebars Bella noticed there was something heavy in the right pocket. Thinking this might be a tool of some kind, she asked: "You don't have a spanner, do you?" Light shook his head. He took hold of Bella's bicycle and wheeled it into the road. He examined it and hand-tightened a bolt. "Yeah, it needs a spanner really, but this should do you." He passed back the bicycle: "Looks like we're going the same way."

Bella's heart sank further. "I'm visiting friends," she remarked, hoping to dissuade him from accompanying her, "I won't be any company at all." The ruse failed. Without saying anything, Ronald Light cycled alongside. Her spirits rose when he stopped to attend to his rear tyre again. She cycled on, hoping to be rid of him, but he soon caught up with her.

Light tried to make conversation. "My tyre's in a bad way. It's so porous. I should have replaced it ages ago, but you know how expensive they are these days." Bella made no comment. "You work at a tyre factory – don't you get them at cost price?"

"I guess that's one advantage of working there," she sighed.

7:25pm. "That's a grand-looking church," Light remarked. "What's this village?"

"Gaulby."

The couple cycled past St Peter's church, with its ornate pinnacles rising from each corner of the tower, and rode on down a hill lined with a several semi-detached houses. Bella slowed. "There is my uncle's cottage," she said, gesturing to a red-brick house a dozen yards away. "Goodbye."

Pulling his bicycle to the far side of the road, Light decided to wait. This was too good an opportunity to squander. His previous attempts to be alone with Bella had always failed. When he saw her she was always with friends, or cycling near to home, and there was never sufficient time to strike up the appropriate conversation. But he had always seen that look in her eye; there was no mistaking what it meant. Now there was an entire journey home to spend together, just him and her. He was certain that would be all he needed to make something happen between them.

8pm. On seeing the old bearded man appear at the cottage window like a grumpy troll, Light decided wisely to cycle on. He freewheeled to the bottom of the lane and turned right to head back towards St Peter's church and the Leicester road, which he knew Bella would have to take for her homeward journey. To ensure the bicycle did not play up on the important journey home he pumped up the tyres. And waited.

8:35pm. Where was she? Becoming impatient and agitated, Light cycled around the church and started the gentle descent to the cottage. By a stroke of luck, as he approached he saw Bella and her relatives standing in the road by the gate.

"Bella," he said to her in a reproachful tone, "you have been a long time." She did not respond.

"That's an unusual colour," Jim Evans remarked, pointing at Light's bicycle. While Bella talked to her relatives Light was happy to talk about his BSA deluxe.

8:45pm. "Well, I'd better be going," Bella announced.

Light muttered, "I'd better put my coat on." He took his khaki-coloured mackintosh, which was slung over his right shoulder, and unfurled it. After Bella had said her farewells, he spun his bicycle around and walked beside her towards the church.

After a few yards, Bella hissed: "Why did you wait?"

"I had a puncture. It took me the best part of an hour to fix it."

"You suddenly got a puncture, did you?" she asked accusingly.

At the top of the hill, Bella wrapped herself in her raincoat to fend off the falling temperature. She cycled on, Light following.

9pm. Bella slowed, pulling her bicycle to the side of the lane beside a large copse. To her left was a gate that led to another lane heading south. Light was tailing her, keeping about 10 yards behind. As she dismounted, Light approached.

"I must say goodbye here," she said assertively, opening the gate. She walked her bicycle through and pushed off. She cycled away at a steady pace. She glanced over her shoulder twice to make sure Light was not following. Light stood by the gate, angered at her dismissive rejection of him. He waited until Bella was about a hundred yards ahead before opening the gate. He walked through and mounted his bicycle, cycling a discreet distance behind.

Aware that he might be following, Bella stopped and looked behind. Light also stopped. She furiously waved at him to go away before continuing. Light resumed his slow pursuit. It was like a scene from Sir Arthur Conan Doyle's *The Adventure of the Solitary Cyclist*, when Violet Smith was tailed menacingly by a male cyclist every time she cycled to a train station. The cyclist turned out to be concerned for Violet's safety on a dangerous stretch of road from which she was eventually kidnapped. There was no such guardian for Bella Wright.

As Bella turned the corner into the Via Devana, she glanced right and saw Light was continuing to tail her. Anxiously, she dismounted and hurried through another gate, leaving it open. Remounting, she increased her speed. The road dipped and after she crested the hill, she glanced over her shoulder. She could not see her stalker and, thinking she was rid of him, she slowed.

Light had stopped before the turning, cunningly keeping out of sight, brooding. Months ago, when he had seen Bella for the first time, she had smiled and said "Hello." Like all narcissists, Light believed it was a special smile, just for him. And it had led to obsession. He had pursued her ever since – waiting for her to come home from the factory, or cycling along the rural lanes near Stoughton in the hope of seeing her. He had heard the stories – that she had been intimate with many men – and this made him even more covetous.

As he waited by the turning, he began to stew in misogynistic bile. If she was easy, he told himself, he could take what he wanted. He was never going to have a better opportunity. This was a lonely lane, the perfect place. It was now or never. He was intoxicated by the anticipation of the chase and the knowledge that she would have to submit to his will. It was this sense of power that had to be gratified, as much as his sexual drive. Both flowed from the same well of animalistic and primeval feeling. He turned the corner, manoeuvred through the open gate and began to pedal furiously.

9:10pm. Bella crested another small hill, and started to freewheel down the gentle slope. Towards the bottom she started to pedal again. About 200 yards from a fingerpost pointing to Stretton Parva, she felt a loss of power, as if the chain had become disconnected. "Damn that freewheel!" she muttered to herself. She dismounted and pulled the bicycle over to the grass verge by a wooden gate. She placed her left hand on the saddle to steady her machine and crouched down to inspect the rear wheel. Seconds later, riding like a bat out of hell, Ronald Light came over the brow of the hill. She hurriedly tightened the freewheel as best she could and stood up, but it was too late. He had reached her. Fear tore through Bella as Light threw his bicycle on the ground and rushed towards her.

"Thought you could get away, did you!" he growled, grabbing her left breast. She stepped backwards, her bicycle falling to the ground.

"Leave me alone!" she shouted. As she desperately tried to prise his hand away, he started kissing her. "Get off!" With rising panic she realised his other hand was fumbling with her skirt, and then it was between her legs. "No!" she screamed. She slapped his face as hard as she could and pushed him in the chest. He staggered back. "My Archie's a stoker. He'll sort you out, all right, you vile creep!"

Enraged that Bella was not like a compliant schoolgirl, hate consumed Light, but he felt alive with the power coursing through his veins. He could still take her, still dominate her. Pulling out his revolver from his coat pocket he pointed it directly at her head. Bella reacted immediately, raising her left hand in front of her face, as if defending herself against a blow, and instinctively turned her head away from the gun. Her scream – shrill and full of terror – was caught in her throat when the bullet hit her. She dropped to the ground like a log, falling backwards.

Although there had been a vicious kick of recoil, there had been no thunderous report as Light was expecting. Rather, the bullet had fizzed out of the barrel like a firework. Now an awful silence descended, only broken by a soft clicking as the back wheel of Bella's bicycle continued to spin slowly. Still holding the gun in front of him, Light stared at the scene. Cautiously, he walked to the body, which was lying at an angle in the road, and bent over it. Bella's brown eyes were fixed in a lifeless stare and fingers of blood were creeping from underneath her hat. There was no hint of remorse: it had been her fault. Rather, he felt empowered and satisfied.

A deep bellow, like the tolling of a bell, echoed across the fields. Replacing the revolver in his coat pocket, Light turned and rushed to his bicycle. He knew that if he wanted to avoid the gallows he had to keep off the road. He flung open the gate but was mindful to close it behind him. He mounted his bicycle and rode like a demon to a stile in the back hedgerow, leaving a track in the grass. Picking up his bicycle, he scrambled over and tore along a narrow footpath which cut through the cornfield. He pushed his way through the tall stems that closed around him like an angry crowd, obstructing and jostling, covering his head and clothes in dust.

He soon approached Stackley House, one of the most impressive manors in the locality, and reached a track that skirted around its land. Turning right, he raced down the path until he hit Stretton Road, which linked Stretton Parva with Great Glen to the south. Dropping his bicycle onto a grass verge, Light stopped to take a breather and tried to compose himself. Aware that he was dusty, he brushed his clothes down as best he could.

Like an ominous harbinger, several horseshoe bats fluttered overhead, effortlessly catching insects on the wing. Light remounted his bicycle and headed home.

Members of the Cold Case Jury, this reconstruction assumes Ronald Light murdered Bella and then fled across fields before reaching Stretton Road. After dusting himself down, he headed south towards Great Glen and then west to Leicester. What evidence is there for this?

Unknown but to a handful of individuals, a belated witness allegedly came forward shortly before the trial to state that he and his fiancée had seen Light on Stretton Road on the night of 5 July 1919. The source of this information is none other than PC Alfred Hall. Long after the trial he wrote an unfinished memoir about the famous case in which he was intimately involved. The memoir was in the possession of his niece and then given to a Leicester law professor, who passed a copy to me. It consists of 16 sides of typed notes and a long poem, a verse of which was published in the Leicestershire and Rutland Constabulary quarterly magazine commemorating his death in 1966. This magazine also referenced the existence of his case notes, in which he tells the following story.

One Sunday, shortly after Light's committal hearing, the constable was visited at his home by Alfred Johnson, a tenant farmer, who brandished a newspaper. He was agitated and pointed to a picture of Light in that day's the *News of the World*. He was certain he had observed the same man on the night Bella died. He explained that he had left home at 8:30pm to make the usual inspection of his fields. He first called on his fiancée, May Walker, who accompanied him on his rural rounds.

During the walk they turned into Stretton Road, heading north towards Stretton Parva. A little later, by a bend, they observed a bicycle lying on the grass verge and, standing next to it, a man in a mackintosh rubbing down his clothes. When the stranger heard them approach, he looked up. The couple had a clear view of his face. At the time they thought nothing of it and walked through a wooden gate into the next field. They saw the man pick up his bicycle, mount it, and cycle at speed towards Great Glen. It was only when Johnson saw Light's photograph in the Sunday paper that he realised whom he had seen on the night Bella died. Hall told Johnson to remain at his house while he verified the story with his fiancée, which he did.

Hall was angry. He had separately interviewed both Johnson and his fiancée after the handbills had been circulated and both failed to mention the incident. They emphasised that they had not seen the colour of the bicycle, which was lying in the grass. Everyone was talking about a green bicycle and they did not make the connection to what they had seen that night. They believed a man had merely fallen from his bicycle and was dusting himself down.

This did not placate Hall, who knew his superiors would think he had messed up the original interviews. Hall informed

Superintendent Levi Bowley, who told the constable that the late identification was "quite useless" and would be prejudicial if it became known publicly before the trial. The couple were sworn to silence. So was Hall, until he wrote his memoir.

Hall's claim cannot be corroborated: there is no mention of Alfred Johnson anywhere in the official police file. Further, the memoir itself is unreliable. Possibly written many years after the events, it contradicts Hall's testimony at the time and is riddled with inaccuracies, not least of which is the fact that there was no picture of Ronald Light in the *News of the World* prior to the trial {see *Exhibit 8*}. But as we shall see in the next chapter, the Johnson story is consistent with a most surprising source.

The reconstruction makes a second assumption – Ronald Light was infatuated with Bella Wright and this led to a sexual assault and murder. What evidence is there for this? We are particularly interested in knowing whether Light had a predisposition for violence and making unwanted advances towards women. We know that Light was expelled from his school for inappropriate behaviour with a young girl, and might have assaulted a French postmistress while he was in France. Is there any other evidence?

In September 1918, Light was invited home for tea by an ambulance driver who worked at the hospital where Light was being treated for war-inflicted deafness. Light not only enjoyed the supper but also the driver's 15-year-old daughter, to whom he made indecent advances. The father reported the incident to the authorities, although no charges were brought.

Chapter 8

In July 1919, as we know already, Light allegedly approached two schoolgirls hours before Bella Wright was killed. No indecent behaviour occurred, but the girls were frightened by his strange manner. Either the girls lied about the meeting or they correctly identified him. A genuine error seems unlikely here. After all, how many other unshaven men riding a green bicycle carrying a mackintosh could there have been? They might have been mistaken about the date, making it harder to draw inferences about his possible state of mind on the night. However, it remains an indicator of his general predisposition.

In October 1919, three months after the death of Bella Wright, Light was questioned by Leicestershire Constabulary over allegations of improper conduct with an eight-year-old girl (as an aside, the police constable failed to match Light to his description in the handbills). Light apologised to the girl and her family, who did not press charges.

All of these incidents suggest that Light was predatory towards young girls. There is no evidence, however, that he was violent, and certainly nothing to indicate he was capable of murder. Of course, his sexual assault and murder of Bella in the reconstruction is purely conjectural, and it is for you to decide how consistent it is with his prior behaviour.

Is there any evidence of Light's possible infatuation with Bella? Sally Ward was the sister of Archie, Bella's boyfriend. According to Wendy East, Bella had told Sally that occasionally a man waited for her in Shady Lane as she returned home, describing him on one occasion as "the soldier that waits for me". The attention was never welcomed. If this man was indeed Light, there is some basis for thinking that he knew Bella, and possibly quite well, judging by how he had spoken to her in front of her relatives. Apart from this, there is nothing to suggest that the victim and the accused knew each other.

The reconstruction was intentionally ambiguous as to the calibre of Light's revolver. Even if we assume that a large-calibre bullet did not cause Bella's death, as Marshall Hall argued, this does not eliminate Light as a murder suspect. There is an interesting fact about the Webley & Scott revolver: it could be fitted with a sub-calibre adapter for use with .22 calibre ammunition. Wendy East suggests that, if Light owned such an adapter, he could have fired smaller calibre rounds. Alternatively, he might have possessed a smaller calibre revolver. Indeed, when he was arrested at Dean Close School, the police found just this type of weapon in his room along with some ammunition. A police report itemised these:

Small revolver ammunition. Belonging to school. Light was in charge of school armoury.

Small revolver. Taken from a schoolboy by headmaster and handed to Light.

Presumably, the police were satisfied that this was not a weapon Light had brought with him from Leicester. Of course, a thriller writer would see it differently: Light took the revolver to school and smuggled it into the armoury as the perfect way of disposing of the murder weapon without suspicion! But we must ignore the plot twists of thrillers. The important fact is that Light might have shot Bella Wright using small-calibre ammunition, which appears more likely to have inflicted the described wounds.

To accept this hypothesis, however, you must also accept that the .455 calibre bullet discovered near the body was completely unconnected to the case. This leads to another question. Assuming that he did use another weapon, why did Light then dispose of his .455 calibre ammunition? There could be a simple answer: because it had been widely reported that such a bullet had been found at the scene, and he did not want to have any connection to the case.

Most writers who uphold the murder theory, such as Russell Wakefield and Wendy East, believe that Bella Wright was lying on her back looking upwards when Ronald Light stood to her left and fired downwards. Both writers believe that such a prostrate position best explains the bullet's trajectory through Bella's head. Also, a shot fired so close would explain why there might have been stippling on Bella's cheek. However, unless Bella was unconscious when Light fired, it suggests she "almost posed for the shot", to quote Marshall Hall. In fact, Bella was found lying partly on her left side, making it impossible to inflict the wounds with the body in this position. So another assumption must be added, the most likely being that Light rolled the body after he had killed her, although it is difficult to see what would be gained from such an action.

In my reconstruction, however, I present a different view based on the premise that Bella's head, and not the line of fire, was angled, producing identical head wounds {see *skull diagram, Exhibit E*}. This is consistent with the fact that most revolvers are held horizontally when fired, the barrel being a few inches below the eye-line of the shooter. Further, if Bella's face was also turned to her right, her left cheek would have been directly in the line of fire, explaining the location of the entrance wound. So, Bella standing and adopting a defensive position – hand upraised with head turned away and tilted back – also explains the bullet's trajectory. Further, if Light was positioned only a few feet away, this would also explain why there might have been stippling on Bella's skin. It is an equally good explanation of the ballistic evidence.

There is one final consideration. Murder is the unlawful act of killing a human being with malice aforethought, which is usually interpreted as having an intention to inflict (at least) serious harm. How do we know that Light intended to kill? If Bella had been on the ground when Light stood over her and cold-bloodedly shot her, it rules out manslaughter immediately. But, if Bella was standing by her bicycle, how can we be sure it was not manslaughter? Perhaps Ronald Light shot her unintentionally. This scenario has never been seriously considered before. And it involves dramatic evidence that has been secreted away in a police safe for nearly a century.

Chapter 9

A SAFE CONFESSION

In *The Green Bicycle Murder,* Wendy East writes:
There is a persistent rumour, again totally unsupported by the evidence, that a signed confession was made by Light and salted away carefully in a police safe in Leicester, where more than one serving police officer in later years claimed to have seen it. None of them, sadly, could produce it.

Rumour is the parent of exaggeration and misinformation, yet often there is also a hard kernel of truth. So it is in this case. There was no confessional statement signed by Ronald Light, but there appears to have been a revealing conversation between the loquacious Light and the assiduous Superintendent Bowley within days of the trial's end. Bowley then provided a written statement of the conversation, which eventually ended up in a police safe. It is a crucial piece of evidence to be placed before the Cold Case Jury.

For many decades this confessional report remained hidden from public view. The complete document is now published for the first time {see *Exhibit 9*}. Based on the confessional report, the following is a reconstruction of the conversation between Light and Bowley about the death of Bella Wright. Its revelations may alter your view of the case. Its significance and Light's motivation for supposedly telling all are entirely for you to judge.

11am. The ample frame of Superintendent Bowley approached the front desk of the county police station in Leicester. "Hello, Mr Light."

"I've come to get my belongings," Light explained in his high voice.

"I'll take it from here, Sergeant." Turning his attention to Light, Bowley said, "I have your personal effects in my room. Follow me." As they walked down the narrow corridor the superintendent added: "I guess congratulations are in order – not everyone escapes a murder charge like the one you were facing."

"I was expecting the verdict, but it was still a great relief to me and my mother."

"Take a seat," Bowley said, leading Light into his small, brightly lit office. He made a point of firmly closing the door behind them and pointed to a box on his desk. "There you are." Light took the box and removed his gold pocket watch and chain. After winding the watch and setting the correct time, he affixed it to his waistcoat. He then picked up the rest of his possessions – some cash, a postal order, a book of postage stamps, a fountain pen and a cheque book – placing them in various jacket pockets.

From his top drawer the superintendent took out a cigarette packet and a box of matches. "Would you like a smoke?" After Light nodded, he slid them across his desk. "I lost count of how many times I gave you some smokes when you were in my custody."

"I appreciated it, old sport," Light said, taking out a cigarette.

Bowley passed an ashtray: "Do you know what?"

Light frowned, striking a match. "What?"

"I'm the only officer here who thought you were innocent."

"That surprises me!" Light lit the cigarette. "I thought you all had it in for me."

"Well, I don't think you murdered that girl at all."

"Fortunately for me, the jury agreed with you," Light joked, blowing out the match and dropping it in the ashtray.

"But there's one thing I can't swallow."

"Oh?"

"You would have never let the woman part from you like that. You like girls too much, Ronald!"

"I guess I do," he smiled, exhaling a column of smoke.

"You've got a history for this kind of thing. We both know that."

"I guess that's true, too."

"So what happened? I swear whatever you say will not leave this room."

"Come on, Superintendent, you know better than that."

"I know you didn't murder her, so what happened? If you don't tell the truth, everyone who ever hears about this case will think you're guilty. You know that don't you?"

"But I was acquitted by a jury of my peers."

"They will still think you did it, all the same. They will say,

ABOVE A large crowd gathers in the early morning for the trial of Ronald Light, which was billed as the most fascinating murder mystery of the century. BELOW LEFT The anguished parents of Bella, Mary Ann and Kenus Wright, walk to court to see Ronald Light tried for the murder of their daughter. BELOW RIGHT Superintendent Taylor (centre) and Superintendent Bowley (left) arrive at court. Days after the trial, Bowley would have a startling conversation with Ronald Light, which he documented in his famous statement

LEFT **PC Alfred Hall** (right) discovered the bullet in the road. He was commended for his role in the case. Sgt. William Healey (left) fished the revolver and cartridges from the canal.

BELOW Looking down, Light appears pensive during his trial. In front of him are his legal team. Behind him, his mother looks on, as do the packed crowd from the gallery.

ABOVE Joseph Cowell (left) discovered the body of Bella. Other witnesses in the picture include Albert Davis and Sidney Garfield of BSA Cycles, the makers of the green bicycle. BELOW Harry Cox (left), the bicycle dealer who repaired Light's infamous green bicycle, poses after giving evidence in court. Enoch Whitehouse (right) found the green bicycle in the canal, which led to the arrest of Light.

ABOVE Bella visited her uncle George Measures (right) on the night she was killed. His son-in-law Jim Evans (left) was an invaluable witness, describing the green bicycle in detail to the police.

LEFT Dr Williams leaves court after giving his testimony. His initial cause of death was inaccurate. George Measures stands in the doorway.

'That Ronald Light, he got away with murder!' Friends of mine said that very thing at the weekend." Bowley waited for his words to sink in before playing his psychological ace. "Why not get this off your chest? Then you can forget all about it, knowing you've done the right thing by telling someone the truth. And you'll feel better for doing it. After what you've been through, surely you owe yourself that?"

Light leaned forward and tapped his cigarette over the ashtray. "If I tell you, can I depend on you to keep it to yourself?"

Bowley tried hard not to show his delight at reeling in his catch. "I've already told you that."

"Whatever I say is strictly confidential. No one else must know. And I'm not signing anything. If you divulge what I tell you, I will just deny it."

"Of course, I understand. It's just between the two of us."

Light leaned back in his chair and took a long draw from his cigarette as he played pensively with the box of matches. Bowley said nothing, hoping his ploy would work. When Light finally spoke there was no preamble, he simply dropped his bombshell.

"Well, I did shoot the girl, but it was completely accidental. We were cycling together and I was telling her about my experiences in France. I said, 'I have my revolver with me, do you want to see it?' She said she did, so we dismounted to look at it."

"This would be by the field gate, along the Via Devana?"

Light nodded, taking another drag from his cigarette. "I had fired off some rounds in the afternoon – you know, for

Chapter 9

a bit of practice – and had no idea there was a loaded cartridge in it. We were both standing by our bicycles." He paused. "I think she had dismounted to the right of her machine."

"So the bicycles were between you?"

"Yes. I took the revolver from my coat pocket and was handing it to her – I cannot remember if she took hold of it or not, but her hand was outstretched to take hold of it – when it went off. I was horror-struck and frightened. I rode away quickly, going by Great Glen. I saw some courting couples between Stretton and Great Glen, so I slowed down somewhat. You know, I didn't want to draw attention to myself."

"I see," Bowley mused. "There's one thing I don't quite understand, though. How did the revolver go off?"

"I cannot account for it, unless it was fully cocked – the least touch would fire it then. She fell over and never stirred. I knew she was dead."

Bowley fell silent, stroking his moustache. Light's account reminded him of a Kipling novel – he could not remember its title – in which a young girl and a soldier were playing with a revolver. The gun suddenly discharged in the hands of the girl. She could not explain how it had happened; it just went off, that's all she knew. It was only when the veil of smoke cleared that she was relieved to see her companion was unhurt.

The superintendent leaned forward, resting his elbows on his desk. "So, did you know her?"

"I had never seen her before that evening, until she asked me for a spanner. That was quite true."

"Did you tell her that you liked her?"

"I said nothing improper to her at all," Light retorted seriously. He then smiled. "That might – no, probably would – have happened later."

"So, you had no intention of harming her?"

"No. If I had wanted to shoot her, I wouldn't have done it so close to the turning for the village. There were much quieter places."

"Or those little girls?"

"Oh, I don't remember them at all. They must have mistaken me for someone else."

"What about the bullet that PC Hall found?"

"I don't think it's the same one. The bullet would have gone much further, and it could not have struck the ground from how we were standing. If it had struck a tree, it would have buried itself there." Light glanced at his pocket watch. Bowley was concerned that Light was about to end the conversation and moved on quickly.

"When did you throw your bicycle in the canal?"

"October, I think."

"Did you ride it there?"

"No. I unscrewed everything that I could before I left home and walked it to Walnut Bridge. From there I got onto the towpath. I first threw in the mudguards, then the gear case, the chain, the cranks and pedals, until the whole lot was gone."

"And the holster too?"

"Yes, I weighed it down with the cartridges."

"If you had left the revolver inside, that would have sunk it!" Having raised the issue of the revolver, Bowley casually added: "Is that in there, too?"

"No, I had it with me and it was loaded. I was so nervous that had anyone interfered with me I would have shot them. I would have been guilty of murder then!"

"So, where is the revolver?"

"It's in the canal. I threw that and another near to Belgrave Gate."

Bowley paused. Light threw *two* revolvers into the canal? Bowley thought about asking about the make and calibre of each, but he feared that if he pushed too hard Light would become uncooperative and leave. Instead, he changed tack, focusing on whether anyone could corroborate Light's story. "Did your counsel know about it being an accident and everything?"

Light shook his head. "I said I had not been to Gaulby at all, and it was not till later I was persuaded to tell the truth."

"I suppose they said it was no use lying when there were eyewitnesses who had seen you there."

"Quite. So I told them the story you heard in court."

"Did they ask you whether it had been an accident?"

"Yes, but I stuck to my story that I left the girl at the junction of the two roads. If I admitted shooting her, I was sure I would be found guilty of manslaughter."

"You ran a great risk."

Light leaned forward and stubbed his cigarette in the ashtray. "I suppose I did, but I would rather have my neck stretched than do 10 years inside for manslaughter. That's me done. I need to go."

"Can I tell the chief constable?" asked Bowley, conveniently forgetting that the information was supposed to be for his ears only.

"No."

"I think this is important."

"Why? What's in it for me?"

"It's your side of the story, Mr Light. Isn't that important if it's the truth?"

Light stroked his chin as he considered the request. "You can after a while but not now." He stood up to leave.

The superintendent fired a final question at him: "Does your mother know?"

"My God, no! I would not let her know it for the world. No one on this earth knows the truth but us two. If you tell, I shall say I never said anything of the kind."

Bowley moved from behind his desk and opened the door. They shook hands with a nod of acknowledgement, nothing more. Ronald Light left, and would never speak of the green bicycle case again. As Levi Bowley closed the door, the title of the Kipling novel flashed into his mind. Walking to his desk he smiled wryly to himself. It was called *The Light That Failed*.

He sat behind his desk, heaved the bulky typewriter towards him and wound a sheet of paper around the platen. He began typing his statement before the details started to fade.

County Police Station,
14 June 1920
At about 11am this day RONALD VIVIAN LIGHT (who was on the 11th instant acquitted of the murder of ANNIE BELLA WRIGHT at Stretton Parva on 5 July 1919) came to this office...

His statement would not be seen by the public for nearly a century.

Members of the Cold Case Jury, the text of the original document is presented in Exhibit 9. As the reconstruction shows, the key points in the Bowley Statement are:

✤ Light continues to deny knowing Bella Wright and meeting the two schoolgirls.

✤ He had used the revolver for shooting practice and carried it in his raincoat pocket.

✤ The revolver went off accidentally when he was showing it to Bella Wright. Both were standing by their bicycles at the time.

✤ Light suggests that the bullet found in the road was not the one he fired. Interestingly, he justifies this using a précis of the argument used by Marshall Hall at his trial.

✤ Light admits to possessing two revolvers.

✤ He fled the scene by cycling to Great Glen and saw some courting couples on Stretton Road.

Taking the last point, if PC Hall's memoir is to be believed, there was at least one courting couple on Stretton Road at that time: Alfred Johnson and his fiancée. They said Light cycled south to Great Glen. The statement and the memoir are consistent on this detail. Another of Light's claims – the disposal of two revolvers – had never been known before Bowley revealed them. It merits further investigation, which we shall do in the next chapter.

So much for what Light is alleged to have said. It is also important to look at what Light did not say because the confessional is not a complete account. It contains three explanatory holes. First, Light never identifies the revolver that fired the fatal shot. Considering that he later says he disposed of two weapons, we cannot be sure he was referring to a Webley & Scott service revolver. If he was carrying a smaller calibre firearm on the night of Bella's death, would this make better sense of Bella's head wounds?

Second, why did the two cyclists turn off the upper road from Gaulby? It is puzzling that they should be on the Via Devana, adding at least a mile to each of their journeys, when it was getting late {see *Exhibit B for a map of the area*}. Light offers no explanation. Perhaps it was trivial. Or was he hiding the real reason?

Finally, he is equally as vague on the critical issue: how had the revolver fired accidentally? He could not account for the shot other than suggesting the firearm may have been fully cocked when he took it out to show Bella. Light said he had fired some rounds in the afternoon, yet it was late evening when Bella was shot. If "the least touch would fire it", is it plausible to believe that he could carry the revolver in his coat pocket for hours without it going off? This was not a formal interview, and it would be unreasonable to expect a full account of everything that happened. Nevertheless, you should bear in mind that these important questions are left dangling with no answers.

Members of the Cold Case Jury, you now know what was said, and what was not, during the alleged conversation, but there is an even more fundamental question. Light had just been acquitted of murder, so why did he risk telling all, especially to a senior police officer? The confessional occurred just three days after Marshall Hall had given his closing speech to the jury. As Light sat silently behind his defence barrister, watching his every gesture and listening to his every word, he surely would have been interested to hear what Hall said about an accidental death:

There's not a man, woman or child who would not have accepted his story. There was the man's perfect defence… it's practically examination proof.

Whether true or not, perhaps Light believed that claiming it was an accidental death would put the matter to rest for good.

Regardless of the veracity of the Bowley Statement, the manslaughter theory it advocates is worth considering as a potential verdict for the Cold Case Jury. We do not need a confession to realise that such a scenario is plausible. When taking everything into account, is manslaughter the best explanation of Bella's death? Based on the statement, the following reconstruction shows how Light might have accidentally shot Bella Wright.

Let us rewind the years and return to the rural lanes of Leicestershire for the final time. It is Saturday 5 July 1919, and Bella Wright has just half an hour to live.

8:45pm. "Why did you wait?" Bella asked, as she pushed her bicycle up the small hill towards St Peter's church.

"I had a puncture. It took me the best part of an hour to fix it."

"You suddenly got a puncture, did you?" she queried mockingly.

"The rear tyre's in a bad way. It's so porous. I should have replaced it ages ago, but you know how expensive they are these days."

"I can get them at cost price, you know. That's one advantage of working at a tyre factory!" Light was about to ask Bella whether she would be able to procure one on his behalf when she changed the subject. "Do you think it is going to rain? I hope not. I hate cycling in the wet."

He looked skywards. "If anything, the weather looks brighter to the west, but I came prepared." He pointed to his raincoat. "Some summer, eh?"

After cycling approximately a mile from Gaulby, they approached a large copse. There was a distant warbling. "Oh, I love nightingales," Bella enthused. "I could listen to their song all day." She pulled over and stopped by a rickety gate leading to a road on the left. "It's coming from over there." She opened the gate. "Let's see if we can spot it."

Light followed her through, closing the gate behind him. They travelled 50 yards and stopped by an enormous thicket of brambles by the roadside. "It's in there somewhere. Just listen to it. It's like… I don't know… an aria," she said with a giggle. "You know what I mean?"

"Yeah, I do," Light replied solemnly. "I remember hearing this at the Somme. It was dawn during a heavy bombardment that had lasted hours. The shells were still exploding around us and our guns were giving as good as they got. And then above the infernal pounding there came this… this beautiful sound from a nearby copse… it was like… an opera singer, as you say. It seemed impossible that a small bird could defy the artillery. All the lads in the trench stopped what they were doing – none of us could believe it. Some even thought it was a miracle, an omen that the war would soon be over."

"That's a beautiful story," Bella replied. "I shall remember it each time I hear a nightingale." After listening to the birdsong some more, she pointed down the lane. "Shall we continue this way? There will be a turnoff and that will take us back towards Leicester." They pushed off. The lane took them through flat, open pastures of grazing sheep and cattle. In the distance on their left was the limestone tower and balustrades of the King's Norton church. A masterpiece of Gothic architecture, and standing imperiously in its humble surroundings, it looked like a cathedral among the green fields.

The road soon turned by another copse, and not long afterwards, they turned right into the Via Devana. "I guess everybody was afraid, at the Front," Bella commented.

"Everyone was scared at some time – only a liar would say otherwise. The new recruits were the worst, of course. If you survived the first month or so, you quickly became a fatalist."

"That doesn't seem a proper attitude for an officer!"

"It was the only way to stop going crazy. I remember hearing a story about a sergeant who had just returned to duty after his honeymoon. His commander made sure he had the safest position, well to the rear of the forward positions. Shelling was light, but there was this stray shell, totally off target." Light paused. "The poor lad was their only fatality that day."

"Oh, that's terrible!

"Well, they say you never hear the bullet that has your name on it, so there's no point worrying."

"Once your number's up, it's up, I guess." Bella paused, wondering about the propriety of her next question, but she asked it all the same. "Did you kill anyone?"

"When I was a gunner, I probably killed scores, if not hundreds, but I didn't shoot anyone, if that's what you mean." The two cycled in silence for a moment, reflecting on what had been said, then Light added: "Actually, I've got my revolver with me, the one from the war. Do you want to have a look?"

"Yes," Bella replied. "Let's pull over here."

They stopped not far from a wooden field gate by a meadow, and dismounted. Bella stood on the grass verge, her bicycle leaning against her. Light was on Bella's left and a yard or so from her.

"It's not the same as when I had it in France," Light said, steadying his bicycle with one hand and rummaging in his coat with the other. "I've had it adapted..." The revolver muzzle caught on the edge of his pocket as he pulled it out. He tugged, forcing it free, but the gun jerked up and his finger snatched at the trigger. There was a loud crack and Light felt a kick in the abdomen by the powerful recoil. He watched in horror as Bella was thrown backwards and collapsed to the ground like a felled tree, her bicycle crashing in front of her.

Still holding the gun by his waist, Light stared at Bella in disbelief. He was expecting her to sit up, to say something. When she remained motionless and silent, he walked to the body and bent over it. Bella's brown eyes were fixed in a lifeless stare and fingers of blood were creeping from underneath her hat. In total panic, he started shaking. His instinct was to run and say nothing. Who was going to believe the truth, anyway? If he admitted to manslaughter, he would get 10 years. Or worse, having admitted that he had shot her, they would try him for murder – and he would hang.

A deep bellow, like the tolling of a bell, echoed across the fields. He had to make a decision quickly – if he dallied too long, it might be made for him. His instincts prevailed.

They served him well.

Members of the Cold Case Jury, the manslaughter theory has some strong points in its favour. Like the murder reconstruction, it suggests Bella Wright was standing by her bicycle when she was shot, which would account for the relative positions of the body and the bicycle when they were discovered by farmer Joseph Cowell {see *large graphic, Exhibit E*}. It also has a plausible explanation for why the cyclists stopped and pulled over – to look at the revolver. Unlike the murder scenario, which submitted that the fatal bullet had a more or less horizontal trajectory, this theory assumes that the gun went off accidentally when it was at waist height and pointing upwards. Both are consistent with the location of the head wounds {see *skull diagram, Exhibit E & Exhibit 3*}.

There is one puzzle with Light's account, however. He says he was handing over the revolver and "her hand was out to take it when it went off". In which case, at the critical moment, how were the two cyclists standing relative to one another and in which direction was Bella looking? The medical evidence shows that the bullet entered Bella's head one inch behind her left eye and exited at the top right of her head {see *skull diagram, Exhibit E & Exhibit 3*}.

This lateral trajectory suggests she was more side on to Light, and not looking at the revolver when she outstretched her hand. Is this the way you would take any object, let alone a revolver? This is an important question to ponder.

There is another possibility. To show off or intimidate her, Light took out his revolver, not knowing there was a cartridge left in the chamber. As he brandished it, Bella reacted, instinctively moving her head away. "Don't point that thing at me!" But it was too late – the gun went off accidentally. Whether he had been reckless, or whether there was a more sinister intent to his behaviour, Light was unlikely to tell this to Bowley.

This leads to another question. How do we know the Bowley Statement is in fact genuine? We have a right to be suspicious of documents suddenly surfacing from the depths of history – just think of the Hitler diaries, which came to light in 1983 and were purchased for millions. They were forged. Suspicions have also been raised over the Bowley Statement. How can we be sure that this statement was not a hoax, perpetrated by a clever forger who wished to rewrite history with his own view of what happened?

In an attempt to answer this question we fast-forward nearly a century to November 2016.

Chapter 10
PRIVATE INVESTIGATIONS

Our story moves to a small, unassuming laboratory in rural Hampshire. It is not a cleanroom with white-coated scientists conducting experiments involving test tubes or space-age technology. It looks more like a normal office, except the worktops are cluttered with specialist equipment. Several people are gathered around a computer monitor connected to an ultraviolet scanner, on which rests a single sheet of yellowing, foolscap paper. It is the first page of the Bowley Statement.

A switch is flicked, a light shines upon the paper, and an image slowly extends down the screen. A forensic document analyst peers intently at it. His name is Robert Radley, who is renowned for proving that the largest contested will in legal history was a fake. He examines the paper's structure on the display to see whether it contains any white fibres, which are used in modern papers to make them brighter. If the paper contains these fibres, it does not originate from the first half of the 20th century; the statement would be a blatant fake.

The analysts continue to stare at the image, scrolling it on the screen. Dotted in the paper are small curved lines like thin worms. After about half a minute, Rob leans back in his chair, removes his spectacles and looks at me.

"What have you found?" I ask, holding my breath.

Members of the Cold Case Jury, the existence of the Bowley Statement was confirmed in 2007 by writer Bill Donahue in an article for *Bicycling* magazine. He found it among papers at the Leicestershire County Records Office, where the archivist told him that the statement "was secret until the Leicester police deposited it with us just eight or 10 years ago". Donahue was suspicious of the statement's authenticity, primarily because its typing was noticeably neater than the other police statements in the case file. He showed his copy to two typography experts. One proclaimed it to be suspicious, while the other thought it was genuine. None the wiser, Donahue left his investigation there, leaving a cloud of doubt hanging over the document's authenticity.

If the document was forged then Light never uttered any confession to Superintendent Bowley. Although this would not mean that the manslaughter theory is false, it would take away the most important evidence to think that it might be true. More needs to be known about the document.

It would be almost impossible to demonstrate conclusively that it is genuine. Rather, the best way forward is to attempt to falsify the document's authenticity, to prove it had not been typed in 1920. To investigate matters further,

Chapter 10

I enlisted the help of a friend with an interest in historical murders. Tall and exuding a natural air of authority, Paul Stickler looks every inch the modern detective. Trained at the FBI headquarters in Virginia, he rose to the rank of chief superintendent with Hampshire Constabulary. Now retired, he researches and lectures on past murder cases. He is also an expert on historical police procedures, providing insight on how the police would have investigated these cases compared to today.

After receiving the permission of Leicestershire Police to undertake forensic tests, the document was taken to Rob Radley, the director of the Forensic Document Laboratory, who kindly agreed to examine it. He first scrutinised the foolscap document with the naked eye. He held it up to the light. "Look at this," he said, "they don't make watermarks like this anymore. This is really beautiful." The paper contained a large translucent image of three crowned owls and the words *Pro Rege et Lege* (for King and Law).

It was discovered later that the watermark was of the Leeds City Council crest. Why was Leicestershire Constabulary using this paper stock? It seemed odd but Paul remained sanguine, explaining that in the early part of the 20th Century, and especially after World War I, police officers would use whatever paper they could lay their hands on. Despite contacting various companies and paper associations, no further details about the watermark could be established. It could not help in dating the document.

What about the typography? Rob immediately dismissed the idea that the neatness of type indicated that a more modern typewriter had been used. Indeed, he showed us an example of uniform typing from a 19th-Century document. He explained that the misalignment of letters is caused by a worn typewriter mechanism, not necessarily by an early typewriter model. Rob could find no typographical evidence to suggest the Bowley Statement was not typed in 1920.

Rob is an expert on signatures, and his work often involves disputed wills. "Where there's a will, there's an unhappy relative," he jokes. This was particularly true when he was called to give evidence about one of the most famous disputed wills in history. When she died in 2007, Nina Wang was the richest woman in Hong Kong, with an estate worth 20 times more than that of billionaire Howard Hughes. She had allegedly changed her will a year before her death and this document – and in particular her signature on it – became a legal battleground. Rob compared her signature on the will to numerous samples of her known signature and discovered a large number of differences. Finding so many divergent characteristics in one signature was extremely improbable, he claimed. His evidence was critical; the judge found that the will was forged.

The signature on the Bowley Statement was compared to two other samples of the superintendent's signature. These were from police reports that the superintendent had signed a year previously. There were a couple of minor discrepancies between them, but Rob explained that no two signatures from the same person are identical. In his opinion, there was nothing to suggest that the signature had been forged.

This led to the last forensic test. If the paper showed the presence of optical brighteners under ultraviolet light, the paper was modern and the document fake. Although the paper contained fibres – the lines I had seen on the screen – they were not white. This meant that the paper was manufactured prior to the 1950s.

The paper stock, the typography and the signature were all consistent with the document being typed in 1920. The discovery of the watermark, although a little unexpected, did not prove the contrary. While these tests are not conclusive, there is no forensic evidence to support the claim that the Bowley Statement is a forgery.

In addition, there is compelling circumstantial evidence of the statement's authenticity. Just days after the Bowley Statement was written, there was a letter from the Director of Public Prosecutions (DPP) to Chief Constable Holmes referenced "Light" {see *Exhibit 10*}. It cites Bowley and a document the chief constable left with the DPP with a view to instigating perjury charges. Perjury, of course, is lying under oath, and Light admitted to Bowley that he had lied in the witness box. At the time the double-jeopardy law was in effect – a person could not be tried twice for the same or similar offence – and, therefore, Light could not have been retried for murder or manslaughter, only perjury.

The matter was so sensitive that the DPP said it should be discussed only in person. Holmes visited the DPP the day after receiving the letter. The subject, timing and references in the letter strongly suggest that perjury charges against Light were being considered. It was never taken further because there was no other supporting evidence. The point for us is this: if the document referenced in the DPP's letter was the Bowley Statement, it is no hoax.

Taken together, the forensic examination and the perjury communiqués are powerful corroboration of the statement's authenticity. Of course, Bowley had intimate knowledge of the case and it is possible that he fabricated the entire conversation. But what would be gained from a high-ranking officer making such a fraudulent statement? And there is a small but important detail in the statement that could not have been known even by Bowley. Light said he disposed of two revolvers into the canal. Why would anyone imagine Light disposed of two when he had only ever admitted to owning a Webley & Scott? It is a surprising inclusion, one that also points to authenticity.

If we rule out forgery and fabrication, the Bowley Statement should be accepted at face value: it records a conversation between the superintendent and Light that took place days after the trial. Assuming it is genuine, there is another question to be answered: did Light tell the truth to Bowley? It is an understatement to say Light's veracity is questionable. His initial statements to the police were all falsehoods. His court testimony contained grains of truth, but only on matters that could no longer be rationally denied, and, if the confessional conversation is to be believed, he perjured himself on the main points of evidence. How do we know the confessional is not more of the same?

Light's account would have greater credibility if it contained an unexpected claim that could be confirmed. As already mentioned, one thing he said is both surprising and potentially verifiable – the two revolvers. If they were recovered from the canal, it would not only be a sensational historical discovery, but would also confirm that Light discarded them as he said he had. The first step would be to identify the most likely location. He said he threw them in the canal near Belgrave Gate, a major road in Leicester. A look at a map shows the sweep of the Grand Union Canal does not come close to the road, but an examination of old city maps reveals an intriguing possibility.

Opposite Abbey Park is an extension of the canal called Basin Wharf that heads towards Belgrave Gate. In 1919 it was 20 metres longer than today, terminating behind a picture house (now a filling station) that stood on the road. The wharf is a short walk from Highfield Street, where Light was living, and his most likely route to the canal would take him down Painter Street, which ran parallel with the wharf (and still does) before it turned towards a movable crane at the wharf's edge. Light could have disposed of any incriminating evidence into the wharf here or at its neck, where it joins the main canal. If Light did indeed throw two revolvers in the canal near Belgrave Gate, this would be the obvious place.

The appropriate authorities have been contacted and, working with Paul Stickler, we hope to conduct a marine search of Basin Wharf. By the time you read this, the revolvers might have been recovered, providing a remarkable denouement to the death of Bella Wright nearly a century after her body was found. Or the search might have failed, the clue of the two revolvers adding to the mystery of this already remarkable case. Updates will be posted on the Cold Case Jury website.

Even if the revolvers are recovered, they would not provide a definitive solution. Although they would confirm his culpability, Light would have been motivated to throw the revolvers into Basin Wharf whether he committed murder or manslaughter – that question would still remain. Was his conversation with Bowley a tissue of small truths to conceal a big lie? Or was the confession an act of contrition by which Light finally came clean?

For the first time, the full story of The Green Bicycle Mystery has been told. The latest evidence, some of it never published before, has been placed before the Cold Case Jury. Three theories have been presented as to how Bella Wright was killed. Each has been discussed. It is time to sum up.

Chapter 11

SUMMING UP

Members of the Cold Case Jury, how was Bella Wright most likely killed? This is the question on which you are being asked to reach a verdict. There are three possible choices:

Misadventure: Bella Wright was shot accidentally by a person unknown

Manslaughter: Bella Wright was killed unintentionally by Ronald Light

Murder: Bella Wright was wilfully killed by Ronald Light

It is possible that Bella Wright was murdered by a person other than Light, perhaps by a spurned lover. But as there is no eyewitness testimony to support this and no author or researcher has provided a serious account of this possibility, I have not presented it as an option for the Cold Case Jury to consider. Rather, you are being asked to look at the evidence that has been presented, decide which of the three theories is the most plausible and then deliver your verdict. There is no inconsistency in thinking that Ronald

Light most likely murdered Bella Wright even if, as the original jury found, there is insufficient evidence to prove his guilt beyond a reasonable doubt.

Sir Edward Marshall Hall often gave a famous peroration when defending a client accused of murder. Indeed, he used it in the trial of Ronald Light. With outstretched hands he would mimic the scales of justice and say:

It may appear that the scales of justice are first weighed on one side in favour of the prisoner, and then on the other against him. Counsel on either side puts the evidence in these scales. As the jury watch the scales, they think for a moment that one scale, and then the other, has the greater weight, and then they are level again so they cannot make up their minds. Then in one scale, in the prisoner's scale, unseen by the human eye, is placed the weight of the presumption of innocence.

For the Cold Case Jury there is no weight of presumed innocence. In this case, you are asked to balance the weights of evidence in three scales according to the different verdicts available, and select the heaviest one. It is no easy task. Although no sentence or acquittal hangs on your collective decision, it will be a verdict in the court of public opinion that frames how people will look upon this case in the future. I suggest there are three key questions you need to answer in making your judgement.

Do you believe that Ronald Light was involved in the shooting of Bella Wright? What connects him directly to Bella's shooting? No weapon was found. No witness placed him directly at the scene where the body was found. If you believe that Ronald Light had no involvement, other than riding with her shortly before Bella's death, then clearly your verdict will be misadventure – she was shot accidentally from a distance. An evidential obstacle to this theory is the finding of tiny metal fragments in Bella's face. If this was stippling, and you should recall this was never confirmed by a forensic pathologist, it suggests Bella was shot by someone positioned within a few of feet of her. This was also the view of Robert Churchill, the ballistics expert who did not testify, but one vehemently denied by Marshall Hall, who was also knowledgeable on firearms.

The most plausible 'shooting crows' theory is that a smaller calibre rifle was used by the accidental killer, not an elephant rifle capable of killing large game. By accepting this you would also have to believe that the .455 bullet found by PC Hall was unconnected to the case – its position in the road so close to the body was sheer coincidence. This was the position of Marshall Hall. If the entrance wound in Bella's check bone was too small to admit a large calibre bullet, then this view would be confirmed. Unfortunately, the size of the wound was not precisely measured during the autopsy, and an important clue buried with Bella Wright.

On the other hand, is the confessional conversation an admission of Light's involvement? This presumes the Bowley Statement is authentic. The forensic analysis shows the document to be consistent with one typed in 1920 and signed by Superintendent Bowley. The communiqués between Chief Constable Holmes and the DPP, about potential perjury charges connected to the Light case, also point to authenticity. If it was fabricated, and the conversation with Light never occurred, details in the statement suggest it could be written only by a person with intimate and exclusive knowledge of the case.

It is frustrating for us that Bowley was not more curious about the two weapons Light said he dumped in the canal. If Light had disposed of a small-calibre revolver, then Marshall Hall's defence falls apart – most of it was directed against the prosecution's assertion that a large-calibre weapon had caused Bella's death – and markedly raises the probability that Ronald Light was the shooter.

If you believe that Ronald Light was involved, there are two possible verdicts: manslaughter or murder. How do you differentiate between the two? It comes down to intent, which is hard to gauge. Light's propensity to lie is not much help. Whether the shooting was accidental or intentional, I suggest Light's reaction would have been identical: depart the scene, deny any involvement and deceive the authorities. This is due to his deeply flawed character. As Marshall Hall said, he was a moral coward.

A question that might bear on your decision is motive. Do you believe that Light knew Bella? It is a fact that nearly four out of every five murdered women in the UK knew their killer, and about one third of all murders are precipitated by arguments. Therefore, if Bella was murdered, she probably knew her killer, and was possibly killed over a dispute of some sort. Light, even in his confessional conversation, was adamant he did not know her. Yet two reliable witnesses, George Measures and Jim Evans, both insisted that Ronald Light had said "Bella" when he first spoke to her.

In his statement to the coroner, Measures says that it was possible that, as he approached the cottage, Light heard Evans address Bella by her name {see *Exhibit 5*}. This was not what Light said in the witness box, however. He testified that he said "Hello", which had been suggested earlier by Marshall Hall in a rare cross-examination of a witness. Another possibility is that Light knew of Bella rather than being familiar with her. But, if that were the case, would you have expected him to wait an hour and address her in the way he did?

If you think that Ronald Light and Bella Wright were strangers then it does not rule out murder, but it does make it a little less likely. This is why Marshall Hall was intent on showing there was no relationship and no motive.

In the murder reconstruction, the motive for murder was connected to a sexual assault. It should be remembered that, while there is no doubt that Light had a penchant for girls, there is no evidence that he was violent against women, the allegation of the French postmistress being a rumour. It also appears that after his trial Light never transgressed again. This is extremely unusual for a sexual offender.

Finally, what do you make of the explanatory gaps in the confessional statement? Do you find it suspicious that Light was unable to fully account for how the revolver went off accidentally? Or is this indicative that Light was actually telling the truth? Events often occur suddenly and we do not know precisely what happened; we have no ready explanation and this makes us appear guilty. Similarly, there is no explanation for why the cyclists were on the Via Devana in the first place. It was getting late and to be certain of reaching her home before nightfall, Bella would have surely chosen the most direct route home. Perhaps there was a reason, but Light did not think it important to mention it, or Bowley forgot to include it in his statement.

Summing Up

It comes back to the Bowley Statement – the remarkable document that has been kept in a safe for nearly a century. If you have not read it already, you soon will {*Exhibit 9*}. Does it have the ring of truth and point to manslaughter? Or does it only confirm Light's involvement but remain unconvincing as to the whole truth? As the confessional conversation was not signed by Light, you can choose to ignore it altogether. This is for you to decide.

With these questions in mind, it is now time to turn to the evidence. In Part Two you will find photographs, diagrams, witness statements, facts and background information. These are not footnotes to the story. They allow us to see the crime scene, hear witnesses in their own words and place events in their full context. Only after seeing the evidence will we be in a position to form an opinion of what happened that summer night a century ago. In Part Three I provide my judgement as to what occurred.

After examining the evidence, I hope you will deliver your verdict on the case. Visit the Cold Case Jury website (**coldcasejury.com**) and simply click on 'Your Verdict' for The Green Bicycle Mystery and follow the simple instructions. After you have cast your vote, you can look at the collective verdict of the Cold Case Jury.

PART TWO

The Evidence

Our story is not yet finished.
It can only be completed by listening
to the narrator of every crime.
The evidence.

What can be asserted without evidence
can be dismissed without evidence.

Christopher Hitchens,
journalist and essayist.

LIST OF EXHIBITS

Images and Diagrams

A   Victim and Suspect
B   Leicestershire Map
C   Stretton Parva Map
D   Shooting Crows Theory
E   Murder and Manslaughter
F   The Bowley Statement
G   The Green Bicycle

EXHIBIT A: Victim and Suspect Did Ronald Light (right) know Bella Wright (left) and call her by her first name? Or was he 'a perfect stranger'?

EXHIBIT B: Leicestershire Map 1919 This scale drawing is based on the map
shown at the trial. The 'Via Devana' was also known as 'Burton Overy Road' and
'Gartree Road'. The 'Upper Road' is also referenced as 'the Leicester road'.

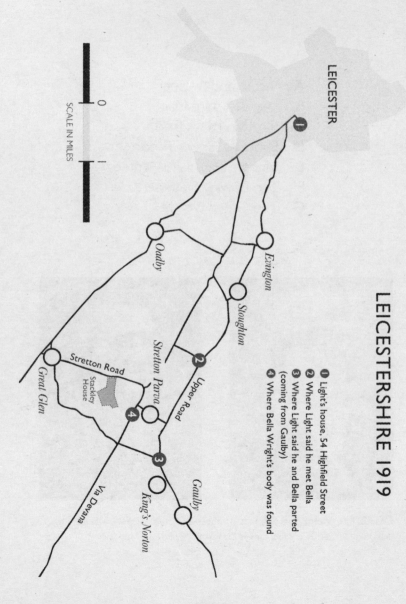

LEICESTERSHIRE 1919

SCALE IN MILES

0

LEICESTER

Oadby

Evington

Sloughton

Great Glen

Stretton Road

Stackley House

Stretton Parva

Upper Road

Via Devana

King's Norton

Gaulby

1 Light's house, 54 Highfield Street
2 Where Light said he met Bella
3 Where Light said he and Bella parted
   (coming from Gaulby)
4 Where Bella Wright's body was found

EXHIBIT C: Stretton Parva Map Based on an original from the 1920s, this map shows the fields to the south of the Via Devana and a footpath that crosses the meadow and the field behind. Was this the track that Cowell pointed out to PC Hall? Was it used by whoever shot Bella to flee the scene unnoticed?

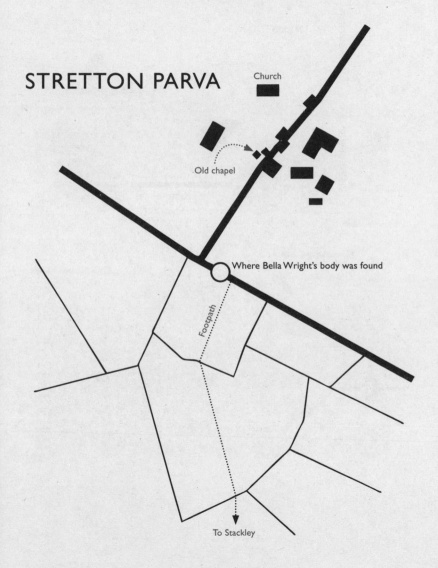

STRETTON PARVA

Church

Old chapel

Where Bella Wright's body was found

Footpath

To Stackley

EXHIBIT D: Shooting Crows Theory A diagram showing how a hunter lying down at the trough in the meadow could have accidentally shot Bella Wright.

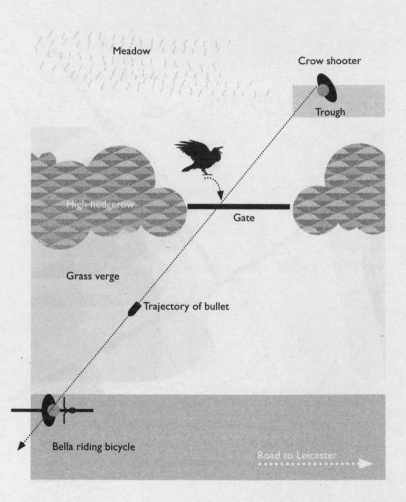

Meadow

Crow shooter

Trough

High hedgerow

Gate

Grass verge

Trajectory of bullet

Bella riding bicycle

Road to Leicester

Exhibit E: Murder and Manslaughter Top: In both the murder and manslaughter reconstructions Bella is standing by her bicycle when she is shot. Bottom: A horizontal bullet trajectory could have also caused Bella's head wounds if her head was tilted at the moment of impact.

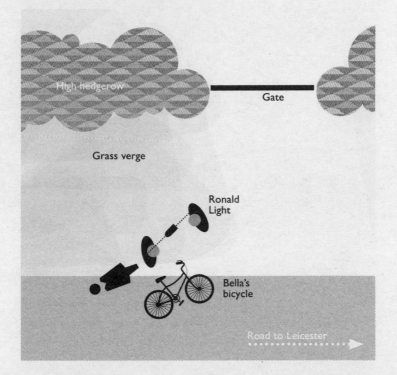

The Effect of Head Position on the Line of Fire: identical wounds in both cases

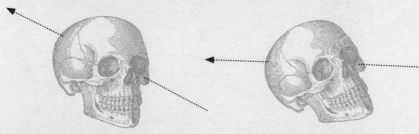

NORMAL: Shot fired upwards   TILTED: Shot fired horizontally

Exhibit F: The Bowley Statement Unseen by the public for nearly a century, does the Bowley Statement provide us with Light's confession or his final deception?

County Police Station,
Leicester.
14th June, 1920.

At about 11 a.m. this day, RONALD VIVIAN LIGHT (who was on 11th instant acquitted of the Murder of ANNIE BELLA WRIGHT, at Stretton Parva, on 5th July, 1919,) came to this Office to arrange for his property to be handed back to him. I talked with him for about an hour-and-a-quarter about his Trial and about the Murder generally. He and I were together in my Office with the door closed. I pointed out amongst other things that I could not swallow his story of his leaving the girl, and how he said he had done, knowing as I did, of his fondness for women and his past history in this respect. I returned to this subject time after time and told him that I did not believe he had wilfully shot her and that I never had believed that of him.

When Light was in my custody I had endeavoured to make him as comfortable as was possible, and had allowed him certain privileges which he missed when on remand at Prison. In consequence of this he was on good terms with me and said, "Well you are a good Sport, if I tell you something can I depend upon your keeping it to yourself"? I said, Yes, strictly. He said, - "Well I'll tell you, but mind it must be strictly confidential, no other person knows it and if you divulge it I shall, of course, say I never told you anything of the kind. He went on to say - I did shoot the girl but it was completely accidental, we were riding quietly along, I was telling her about the War and my experiences in France, I had my Revolver in my Raincoat pocket and we dismounted for her to look at it. I had fired off some shots in the afternoon for practice and I had no idea there was a loaded cartridge in it, we were both standing up by the sides of our bicycles, I think she had dismounted on the right of her machine and that the two bicycles were between us. I took the Revolver from my Coat pocket and was in the act of handing it to her, I am not sure whether she actually took hold of it or not, but her hand was out to take it when it went off. She fell and never stirred, I was horror struck, I did not know what to do, I knew she was dead, I did not touch her, I was frightened and altogether unnerved and I got on my bicycle

THE EVIDENCE

Exhibit G: The Green Bicycle A bystander stares as the infamous bicycle is
carried casually to court for the committal hearings

LIST OF EXHIBITS

Documents

1   Annual Timeline
2   Hourly Timeline
3   Autopsy Findings
4   Police Handbills
5   Inquest Statements
6   The Chief Inspector's Report
7   Trial Minutes
8   Absent Witnesses
9   The Bowley Statement
10 The Holmes Communiqués

EXHIBIT 1: ANNUAL TIMELINE

The following timeline has been compiled for
The Green Bicycle Mystery. It places all of the events
associated with the death of Annie Bella Wright in a
chronological context.

1885
October 19. Ronald Light born in Leicester
1897
Light attends Stoneygate Preparatory School, Leicester
July 14. Annie Bella Wright born near Melton Mowbray,
Leicestershire
1899
Light admitted to Oakham School, Leicester
1902
Light expelled from Oakham School
1904
Bella attends Somerby School, Leicestershire
1906
Light awarded Diploma in Civil and Mechanical Engineering
November 1. Light starts training with Midland Railway,
Derby
1910
Ronald Light employed as an engineer with Midland
Railway, Derby
May 3. Orton Brothers, bicycle dealers in Derby, place order
with BSA for a green bicycle
May 18. Ronald Light pays cash for the green bicycle
June. Green bicycle delivered to Ronald Light via Orton
Brothers

July: Bella leaves school, and enters domestic service for several years

1911
Light is awarded a third-class degree in engineering

1912
April. Light becomes associate member of Institute of Civil Engineers

1914
August. Light dismissed by Midland Railway, Derby
October. Light returns to live at his parents' house in Leicester

1915
February 27. Light commissioned as 2nd Lieutenant, Royal Engineers
March 14. Light attends Royal Engineers' course at Buxton, Derbyshire
July. Light purchases Webley & Scott Service revolver from Major Benton
September 27. Light posted to Royal Engineers' camp at Newark, Nottinghamshire
November 13. 2nd Lieutenant Light sent to France

1916
January 24. 2nd Lieutenant Light transferred back to England (precise reasons not recorded)
July 1. Light stripped of officer's commission (for not being officer material)
August 2. Light gazetted out of service
September 18. Light enlists as a gunner in Honorary Artillery Company

THE EVIDENCE

1917
May: Bella gives up domestic service and works as machinist in Leicester (estimated date)

July 27. A district court martial finds Light guilty of forging War Office telegrams

October 16. Light expelled from Institute of Civil Engineers

November 13. Light sent to France with Honourable Artillery Company

1918
June: Bella tells her mother that an officer has fallen in love with her (see note 1, end of this section)

August 24. Light admitted to Wharncliffe War Hospital for progressive deafness and tinnitus

September: Light molests 15-year-old daughter of ambulance driver

October 22. Light discharged from Wharncliffe War Hospital

1919
February. Light demobilised at Ripon, Yorkshire; Bella starts work at St Mary's Mills, Leicester

Spring. Leicester cycle dealer Walter Franks affixes mudguards to Light's BSA bicycle

July 2. Light visits Leicester cycle dealer Harry Cox to repair his BSA bicycle

July 4. Light returns to Cox to shorten the gear cable on his BSA bicycle

July 5. Farmer Joseph Cowell finds the body of Bella Wright at 9:20pm

July 6. PC Hall finds a spent bullet on the road and a bullet wound in Bella Wright's left cheek

July 7. Autopsy of Bella Wright's body; *Leicester Mercury* runs minor story entitled 'Woman Cyclist's Death'

July 8. Reward handbills circulated by police; 'Stretton Murder Mystery' is the headline in the *Leicester Mercury*; coroner's inquest opens into death of Bella Wright {*Exhibit 5*}

July 9. Cycle dealer Harry Cox tells police he finished repairs to a green bicycle on July 4

July 11. Bella Wright buried at Stoughton Church; PC Hall submits his 6-page written report (see note 2, end of this section); Leicestershire Constabulary call in detectives from Scotland Yard

July 15. New handbills circulated by police, reward increases from £5 to £20 {*Exhibit 4*}

July 25. Second day of coroner's inquest

July 29. Detective Chief Inspector Albert Hawkins of Scotland Yard submits his report

August 8. Third day of coroner's inquest

August 25. Verdict of 'wilful murder' returned by the jury at the coroner's inquest

October 28. Ronald Light admits to improper conduct with a young girl; the girl's family do not wish to bring charges; the police release Light

December. Light throws his dismantled green bicycle into the River Soar canal (see note 3, end of this section)

December 15. Light is accepted for a teaching post at Dean Close School, Cheltenham

1920

January 20. Ronald Light starts teaching mathematics at Dean Close School

February 24. Frame and front wheel of a green BSA bicycle recovered from the River Soar canal

March 1. Cycle dealer William Saunders discovers a hidden serial number on the BSA bicycle

March 2. Detectives speak to BSA Cycles Ltd in Redditch and discover the bicycle was sold to a Derby dealer

March 3. Orton Brothers in Derby tell police that the green bicycle was sold to Ronald Light in 1910

March 4. Ronald Light questioned by police; after formal identification by cycle dealer Harry Cox, Ronald Light is formally charged with the murder of Bella Wright

March 5. Ronald Light identified by George Measures as the man on the green bicycle

March 9. Schoolgirls Muriel Nunney and Valeria Cowan give statements to police

March 10. Committal hearing, first day

March 12. Back wheel of bicycle recovered from canal

March 17. Committal hearing, second day

March 19. Holster and cartridges recovered from canal

March 23. Committal hearing, third day

March 24. Ronald Light sent for trial

March 28. The *News of the World* publishes an account of the committal hearing {*Exhibit 8*}

April 29. Gear wheel pedal and crank recovered from canal

April 30. Pedal with back-peddling brake recovered from canal

June 9. Trial of Ronald Light begins, with Sir Edward Marshall Hall defending Light {*Exhibit 7*}

June 11. Trial ends with acquittal of Light

June 14. Light provides off-the-record confession to

Superintendent Bowley {*Exhibit 9*}
June 16. Light writes to Marshall Hall expressing thanks for his acquittal
June 23. Possible perjury charges against Light considered {*Exhibit 10*}
July 19. Perjury charges against Light abandoned
1934
December 11. Ronald Light, aged 49, marries Lilian Bower, aged 50
1964
July. BBC broadcasts programme about the case as part of its *Call The Gun Expert* series
1975
May 15. Ronald Light dies aged 89.
2016
November. Bowley Statement undergoes forensic document analysis

Notes
(1) According to Mary Wright, Bella's mother, this conversation occurred around a year before Bella's death or earlier.
(2) PC Hall's report has not been included as an exhibit because much of its detail was used in reconstructing events in chapters two and three.
(3) Date provided by Mary Webb, the housekeeper. According to Light's testimony and statement to Bowley, this was at the of October. Nothing hangs on this detail.

EXHIBIT 2: HOURLY TIMELINE

Some of the times stated below are estimates, especially when there is conflicting information for the events concerned. The timeline for PC Hall's activity on the Sunday is taken from his police report dated 11 July and his testimony at the coroner's inquest {*Exhibit 5*}.

Saturday 5 July 1919

14:30. Bella rises after late shift at work and writes three letters

18:10. Bella cycles to Evington, buys stamps from Kathleen Powers

18:30. After returning home, Bella begins her cycle ride to see her uncle, George Measures, in Gaulby

18:45. Ronald Light, on his green bicycle, meets Bella, who has trouble with her wheel

19:15. Farmer Thomas Nourish sees a man and a girl cycling towards Gaulby

19:25. Bella arrives at her uncle's cottage accompanied by Ronald Light

20:10. Joseph Cowell leaves his house to move some cattle

20:15. While Light waits outside, Bella decides to stay longer at the cottage

20:45. Bella leaves her uncle's cottage accompanied by Ronald Light

21:20. Joseph Cowell finds the body of Bella Wright

22:15. Cowell arrives at Great Glen police station saying he has found a dead woman near Stretton Parva

22:30. PC Alfred Hall arrives at the crime scene

23:00. Dr Edward Williams examines the body, believing

death was most likely due to an accident

Sunday 6 July 1919
06:00. PC Hall returns to the scene of the shooting; he finds nothing
08:00. Hall examines Bella's bicycle at the old chapel
10:30. Hall telephones Superintendent Levi Bowley to inform him about the finding of the dead body
11:00. Joseph Cowell interviewed by PC Hall
12:00. Bella Wright reported missing by her mother
15:00. After returning to the scene, Hall finds bloodied claw marks on top of field gate
18:00. Hall returns to the scene for the third time
19:15. PC Hall finds .455 calibre bullet in the road, close to where Bella Wright was found
19:30. Joseph Cowell accompanies Hall to the scene to indicate the exact position of the body when it was found; Cowell notices a single track across the meadow which Hall follows
19:55. Hall cycles to Billesdon to fetch Dr Williams
20:15. Hall washes Bella's face and discovers bullet hole in her left cheek; he waits for Dr Williams
20:40. Dr Williams re-examines body and concludes Bella Wright was killed by a gunshot wound

Exhibit 3: AUTOPSY FINDINGS
Date: Monday 7 July 1919.
Present: Dr E Williams assisted by E Phillips.
Body: Well nourished.
Head: Hair saturated with blood and much blood on face – in nose and mouth.

THE EVIDENCE

A vivid circumscribed bruise, the size of a two-shilling piece (see note 1, end of this section), an inch behind and half-an-inch below level of left eye. In centre of bruise a small puncture wound admitting an ordinary lead pencil, passing upwards, inwards and backwards to another oval wound one-and-a-half inches by half-an-inch over middle and upper third of right parietal bone (2). The brain between the two wounds much lacerated.

There were scratches in left cheek probably caused by gravel.

A contused cut through left upper eyelid, with discolouration of eyeball of left eye. Small incision in left cornea.

Two small contusions between right angle of mouth.

Wrist: Scratches in left hand and wrist.

Genitals: Slight discoloration of external genitals, but no sign of haemorrhage. Hymen absent.

Viscera: All normal. Uterus not enlarged. No other bruising or marks to be found on the body, or signs that any struggle occurred.
The discoloration on left cheek was probably not caused by powder (3).

(signed) E. K. Williams, 22 July 1919

Notes

(1) Diameter: 28.5mm (just over an inch).

(2) About 3 inches above right ear (from PC Hall's report).

(3) There is no reference to tiny metal fragments by the entrance wound. Williams excised and preserved the skin around the wound but also fails to mention this in his report.

Exhibit 4: POLICE HANDBILLS

Two handbills were circulated by the police in connection with the case. The first was dated 7 July, the second 14 July. The differences between the two reflect the changing nature of the case, and the police's frustration at the lack of definite leads by mid-July 1919.

1. The Original Handbill

Telephone 357 and 862

LEICESTERSHIRE CONSTABULARY

£5 REWARD

At 9.20pm, 5th instant, the body of a woman, since identified as ANNIE BELLA WRIGHT, was found lying on the Burton Overy Road (Via Devana), Stretton Parva, with a bullet wound through the head, and her bicycle lying close by.

Shortly before the finding of the body the deceased left an adjacent village in (the) company of a man matching the following description:

✢ Age 35-40 years, height 5ft 7in to 5ft 9in; apparently usually clean shaven, but had not shaved for a few days, hair turning grey, broad full face, broad build, said to have a squeaking voice and to speak in a low tone.

✢ Dressed in light rainproof coat with green plaid lining, grey mixture jacket suit, grey cap, collar and tie, black boots, and wearing cycle clips.

✢ Had bicycle of following description, viz. Gent's BSA bicycle, green enamelled frame, black mudguards, usual plated parts, upturned handle bar, 3-speed gear, control lever on right handle bar, lever front brake, back-pedalling brake worked from crank and of unusual pattern, open centre gear case, Brooke's saddle with spiral springs of wire cable. The 3-speed control had recently been repaired with length of new cable.

Thorough enquiries are earnestly requested at all places where bicycles are repaired.

If met with the man should be detained, and any information either of the man or bicycle wired or telephoned to E. HOLMES, ESQ., CHIEF CONSTABLE OF COUNTY, LEICESTERSHIRE, or to SUPT. L. BOWLEY, COUNTY POLICE STATION, LEICESTER.

County Constabulary Office, Leicester, 7th July 1919

2. The Revised Handbill

Telephone 357 and 862

LEICESTERSHIRE CONSTABULARY

£20 REWARD

MURDER AT STRETTON PARVA

On 5th July 1919

The above reward will be paid to any person giving such information as will lead to the tracing of either the man or the bicycle as described below:

✤ Age 35-40 years, height 5ft 7in to 5ft 9in; apparently usually clean shaven, but had not shaved for a few days, hair turning grey, broad full face, broad build, said to have a squeaking voice and to speak in a low tone.

✤ Dressed in light rainproof coat with green plaid lining, grey mixture jacket suit, grey cap, collar and tie, black boots, and wearing cycle clips.

✤ Had bicycle of following description, viz. :- Gent's BSA bicycle, green enamelled frame, black mudguards, usual plated parts, upturned handle bar, 3-speed gear, control lever on right handle bar, lever front brake, back-pedalling brake worked from crank and of unusual pattern, open centre gear case, Brooke's saddle with spiral springs of wire cable. The 3-speed control had recently been repaired with length of new cable.

The man described took the bicycle to be repaired in the Spinney Hill Park district, Leicester, between 10 and 11am on 2nd inst., called at the Cycle Repair Shop at the same hour on the two following days, and took away the machine about 2pm on the day of the murder.

Any person having knowledge either of this man or the bicycle, is earnestly requested to give information to the undersigned.

E. HOLMES

Chief Constable of Leicestershire

County Constabulary Office,
Leicester, 14th July 1919

THE EVIDENCE

EXHIBIT 5: INQUEST STATEMENTS

The following statements, taken under oath, are from the
official record of the coroner's inquest into the death of
Bella Wright. These are placed before the Cold Case Jury
because they provide the testimony of key witnesses shortly
after the event, when memories were fresh. The statements
were elicited by questioning from the coroner and from
others present, such as the chief constable or members of
the jury. I have reordered the sentences in some statements
to group together those with a common subject. Apart
from that, they are presented verbatim. My commentary is
italicised.

The venue for the first day of the inquest was Joseph
Cowell's cottage at Stretton Parva. It was not unusual to
hold an inquest at a private residence. In this case it was a
convenient location for the coroner and jurors to view the
body, which was still lying in the old chapel. Subsequent
days were held at the village hall in Great Glen.

First Day: Tuesday 8 July 1919

Mary Ann Wright. I am the wife of Kenus Wright, farm
labourer of Stoughton. I identify the body the jury has
viewed as being that of my daughter Annie Bella Wright.

She lived at home. She was single and 21 years of age.
She was employed as a rubber hand at Bates & Co, St
Mary's Mills, Leicester. She used to cycle to and from her
work. She was not engaged to be married but was walking
out with a young man. He is a sailor and stationed at
Portsmouth.

I saw my daughter writing some letters on Saturday

189

afternoon. I saw the envelopes in her coat pocket. Evington would be our nearest post office. Between 6 and 7 o'clock last Saturday afternoon the deceased left home. She said she was going to catch the post at Evington. I did not see her again alive.

Joseph Cowell. I am a farmer and live at the Elms Farm, Stretton Parva. Last Saturday evening about 9:20pm I was driving a herd of cows along the Burton Overy Road *(Via Devana)* towards Stretton Parva. When I got about 200 yards from the turning to Stretton Parva I found a girl lying on the road on her left side with her head towards the centre of the road and her feet towards the hedge. I went to her and found she was bleeding from the nose. There was a large pool of blood close to the body. There was a bicycle close to her. I picked her up. Her head fell back and I felt certain she was dead. I placed her on the grass by the side of the road. I came home and asked my wife to send some men to watch the body while I went for the police.

I telephoned for Dr Williams and then went to Great Glen for Police Constable Alfred Hall. I then helped to remove the body to the cottage where it is now lying. The body, which the jury have viewed, is the body which I helped to remove.

The inquest was adjourned, allowing the deceased to be buried.

Second Day: Friday 25 July 1919
Joseph Cowell (recalled). When I telephoned Dr Williams, I said, "I have found a girl fallen from her bicycle at Little Stretton. She is dead." I fix the time at 9:20pm when I

found the body as I looked at my watch at that time. It was the head of the deceased which was lying in the large pool of blood where I first found the body.

Edward Williams. I am a surgeon and reside at Billesdon. About 10.30pm on Saturday 5 July I received a message by telephone from the witness Joseph Cowell to the effect that he had found a woman dead on the Gartree Road *(Via Devana)* close to Stretton Parva. I said I would come over. I went over in my car and called at Mr Cowell's house. This would be about 11:15pm *(both PC Hall and Joseph Cowell said in their signed police statements that the doctor arrived at 10:40pm).* I was told at his house, where the body was lying. I went in my car to the Gartree Road and when I got about 200 yards from the Stretton turn, going towards Gaulby, I saw several people by the side of the road and a milk float. I got out of my car and found the body of the deceased was in the milk float. Someone told me the deceased had been found on the road with a bicycle by her side.

I got in the float and made a cursory examination of the body and ascertained she was dead. The body was quite warm. She had not been dead two hours. The body was then driven in the float to a house {*the old chapel – see Exhibit C*} in Stretton Parva. I then looked at the road at the place where I was told the body was removed from. I saw one large patch of blood and several smaller ones. I then went in my car to the cottage where the body lay. PC Hall was with me. I again just looked at the body but made no detailed examination. I had no suspicion at that time of any foul play. I considered at that time that the injuries were the result of a bicycle accident.

The next evening, in consequence of what PC Hall told me, I went to Stretton Parva about 8:15pm. I found the deceased's hair saturated with blood and there was much blood on her face and in her nose and mouth but not in her ears. I had the head and face of the deceased washed and I made a detailed examination. I found a punctured wound an inch behind and half-an-inch below the left eye. I probed the wound and found it passed upwards, inwards and backwards, passing through the brain and through a wound of exit over the middle and upper third of the right parietal bone. The entrance wound would admit an ordinary lead pencil. The wound I have just described might have been caused by the bullet produced *(the .455 calibre bullet found by PC Hall)*. I made no further examination that night.

The next day I made a post-mortem examination of the body in conjunction with Dr Phillips of Kibworth. {*To avoid repetition the post-mortem details have been omitted. See Exhibit 3*}.

I found minute portions of gravel right in the skin (of the left cheek) and also some minute particles of metal. There was no evidence that the discoloration was caused by gunpowder. I think the shot was fired from a distance of not more than four or five feet. I cannot form an opinion as what position the deceased was in at the time she was shot. The cause of death was shock following the injuries caused by the gunshot wound. Death would be instantaneous.

The deceased's clothing was in perfect order and there was no evidence of any struggle having taken place or any

attempt at violation. The scratches were compatible with
the theory that she had been shot while on her bicycle or
while in a standing position.

Edgar Vaughan Phillips. I am a surgeon and reside at
Kibworth. In conjunction with Dr Williams I made a
post-mortem examination of the body of the deceased on
Monday 7 July. I have nothing to add to his testimony. I
am satisfied from the condition of the body there has been
no struggle of any kind.
After the medical evidence had been heard the inquest was adjourned.

Third Day: Friday 8 August 1919
Harry Cox. I carry on business at 214 Mere Road,
Highfields, Leicester, as a cycle dealer. On Tuesday 8 July I
went to the County Police Station and gave information
after reading a description of a bicycle in the local
newspapers in connection with the murder of a girl at
Stretton Parva.

I recollect that between 10 and 11am on Wednesday 2
July a man called at my shop with a bicycle. He said, "I
want my three speed adjusting." I looked at the bicycle and
said, "I will get it done for you on Thursday."

I had half an hour's talk with him and he said he was
staying with friends in Leicester. He told me he was a
demobilised officer and working for a firm in London. The
firm, he said, had told him he could have another two or
three weeks holiday on full pay as they were not very busy.
He told me he had also a BSA motorcycle.

From the way he spoke I should say he was a Londoner.

He spoke with a cockney accent fairly quickly. He had a squeaky voice. I should say he was 35 to 40 years old, about 5 feet 7 inches to 5 feet 8 inches in height. I should say he worked indoors, his complexion was sallow, hair dark turning grey. He was clean-shaven and had very dark skin where he had shaven. I did not notice the colour of his eyes. His nose was ordinary. His was a big full face. He had on grey flannel trousers and a tweed 'sports' coat. It was not shabby. He had a soft felt hat, an 'Alpine' hat.

The next day he called between 10 and 11am. I told him I had broken the cable. He said, "Put me *(in)* a new one." I told him it would be ready on Friday. He was only in my shop about five minutes. He was dressed the same as the previous day. I put in 4 feet 7 inches of new cable wire. It was a bright silver coloured wire. The back tyre had a John Bull sticking patch placed on the inside and a piece of outer cover patched on a weak place.

On Friday he called about 11am. He was dressed the same as Wednesday. He took the bicycle away and brought it back about 4 o'clock that afternoon and asked to have another inch taken out of the cable so that he could adjust it himself.

On Saturday he called between 1.30 and 2.00pm. He had on a raincoat, khaki drill colour. Just before he left my shop he said he was fed up messing about the town and he was going to have a run out in the country. He rode off in the direction of Old Evington.

I agree with the description of the bicycle which has been circulated by the Leicestershire police with the exception of the mudguards which I did not notice. The bicycle was a 1909 pattern.

Many writers are struck by the fact that Light lied about his place of residence and work. Was his deception evidence that he was planning the murder? I believe the reason is more prosaic: Light did not want to admit that he was an unemployed, court-martialled ex-soldier living off his wealthy mother. As a narcissist, truth was a disposable commodity, to be used and thrown away when it suited. Light would have exaggerated or lied to make a better impression on others.

James Evans. I live at Maltby near Rotherham and am a miner. On Saturday 5 July I was staying with Mr Measures at Gaulby and at about 7:30pm the deceased came over on her bicycle. I had never seen her before. She left her bicycle by the front gate. In about 10 minutes I looked out of the window and I saw the head and shoulders of a man. He was standing 30 to 40 yards from the house. I had never seen him before. I said to Bella, "Who is the stranger in the lane?" She replied, "He is a stranger to me. I picked him up on the road."

Some little time afterwards I went into the lane. I could not see the strange man. I then went back into the house and said to Bella, "I think he has gone." She said, "I shall wait a bit longer." A little while afterwards I was tightening the freewheel of her bicycle and the man rode up on his bicycle. He got off and he said, "I thought you had gone the other way, Bella." She made no reply. I was not looking at her face.

The description of the bicycle circulated by the police is an accurate description of the bicycle which I examined at

Gaulby belonging to the strange man. I have no doubt the bicycle which Mr Cox repaired *(from the description he gave me)* was the same machine as I saw the strange man with at Gaulby on 5 July. I have never seen a bicycle with such a complicated back brake.

Shortly afterwards, Bella and the strange man went off together. They were walking and pushing their bicycles as they went away. I went into the house and said to my wife, "They must have known each other before." If I heard the man speak and he had his back to me I would recognise his voice. His voice was a squeaky one and a high-pitched one. I should say he was nearly 40 years of age, 5 feet 7 inches to 5 feet 9 inches in height, dark complexion and sallow, big face round and full, broad built. He was a clean-shaven man but had two-to-three days growth on his face of black hair. He was dressed in a dirty grey suit which looked shabby but fitted well. He had a fawn-coloured mackintosh over his shoulder.

Evans states that Light said "Bella" at the end of his greeting, rather than at the beginning. If Evans had maintained this position at the trial it would have been difficult for Marshall Hall to suggest that Light had said "Hello" instead of "Bella" (see Chapter 5).

George William Measures. I am a roadman and live at Gaulby. The deceased is my niece. On Saturday 5 July she came to my house on a bicycle. She arrived about 7:15pm. She left her bicycle close to my cottage gate. She stopped, talking with me, until about 8:30pm.

The carrier Charles Palmer called about 7:15pm. I went

to my cottage door and noticed a strange man about 40 or 30 yards up the road. I did not see a bicycle. I did not like the look of him. I turned into the cottage and I said, "Bella, there is a strange man up the road and the carrier does not know him." She said, "He overtook me and said he came from Great Glen, and wanted to know the name of this village."

About 8pm I went to my cottage door and I saw the same man walking up and down the village street. I said to Bella, "That man is walking up and down the street now. He is a strange man and I don't like the look of him." She said, "I will try and give him the slip." She said it in a joking way. She said, "The man is a stranger to me." Bella was then standing against the fireplace ready to go. She said, "I will sit down (for) a few minutes and perhaps he will be gone."

She sat there until about 8:15pm. She again got up to go and went outside to her bicycle. The strange man came down the village street pushing his bicycle. He came just outside the gate. He said, I think, "Bella, I thought you had gone the other way." I think he called the deceased "Bella" after he heard Mr Evans call her that. I did not hear her make any reply. I never spoke to the man.

I only heard him call her "Bella" once. I don't think she would object to being called by her Christian name. I thought he was a stranger to her and I think so now.

I saw the deceased and the strange man leave about 8:45pm.

Margaret Louisa Evans. I am the wife of James Evans. The last witness is my father and on Saturday 5 July I was staying with my father at Gaulby. I recollect the deceased riding over on her bicycle about 7:15pm that night.

I remember my father going to the cottage door. He said, "That man is still up there. He must be waiting for you, Bella." She replied, "I don't know the man. He's overtaken me on the way. He told me he had come from Great Glen and wanted to know the way to some place." My father said, "He is waiting up there and looks as if he is waiting for you." She said, "I will wait a few minutes and see if he goes." She got up and then sat down again.

My husband also said, "There is a man up there, and he looks as if he is waiting for you." My father said, "He looks old enough to be your father." Bella just laughed. All this time Bella was sitting down and could not see the man in the road.

About 8:30pm Bella got up to go and went outside the cottage gate. I went with her. I saw a strange man walking towards the cottage and pushing a bicycle. He walked straight up to Bella. He said, "You have been a long time. I thought you had gone another way." She made no reply. She blushed and looked a little confused. She gave me the impression she did not want to have anything to do with the man.

Bella came in the house for a spanner. My father said, "I don't like the look of that man. I would make haste home." Bella said, "I shall soon get in front of him." I said to Bella, "Now, Bella, do you really know that man." She said, "I do not know the man, he is a perfect stranger to me."

Bella left about 8:45pm with the man, pushing their bicycles. I watched them from the door. They appeared quite friendly. I said to my husband, "Bella must have known the man before." My husband said, "Yes, of course she does."

I should know the man again if I saw him *(later, she failed to pick out Light from a line-up)*. I should say he would be quite 40 years old, five feet seven inches or eight inches *(in)* height, hair dark turning grey, his complexion was pale. I should say he worked indoors or down a pit. He certainly did not work in the open. Clean-shaven and dark skin where he had shaved; he had dark eyes. He was a broad-built man. He was *(a)* big, full-faced man; he had a big nose. He spoke quickly with a cockney twang. He was dressed in a grey suit and a grey cap. I could not say if the suit was shabby. He had a mackintosh rolled up and tied with string across one shoulder and under his arm. The lining was a green check one. The man had a very brazen look.

Henry Clarke. I am a gunsmith and reside at Leicester. I have examined the bullet *(found by PC Hall)*. In my opinion, it is an old pattern .455 calibre. It may be used either for a revolver or rifle. It was fired with black powder. If fired from a revolver, that revolver was a large one and the size of a service one. From the marks on the bullet, it is quite consistent with it having been fired from a rifle.

I would expect no scorching on the face if the bullet had been fired from a distance of 15 yards. There would be scorching whatever the condition of a revolver if fired from a distance of five feet. If fired beyond five feet it would be impossible to say without seeing the weapon.

If the bullet had been fired from a revolver of average

(barrel) length at a distance of 50 or 60 yards it would go right through a person's head; if from a short barrel revolver, 25 to 30 yards.

There are five marks of rifling on the bullet. The other marks and indentations on it, in my opinion, were caused by the bullet striking the road or some other hard substance. It is quite possible that the bullet might have struck the road or some other hard substance and ricocheted and then passed through the head of some person.

Alfred Hall. I am a police constable in the Leicestershire Constabulary stationed at Great Glen. I was on duty on the London Road in the parish of Glen Magna *(Great Glen)* when the witness Joseph Cowell drove up to me. He said, "I have found a young woman lying dead by the side of her bicycle on the Burton Overy Road *(Via Devana)* in the parish of Little Stretton *(Stretton Parva)*." He said a lady's bicycle was lying in the road by her side, and he said, "I think she has fallen off her bicycle. I have picked her up and I found she was dead."

I asked Mr Cowell to go at once and telephone Dr Williams. I went and fetched my bicycle and rode to Little Stretton. Mr Cowell had described to me where the body was lying. I found the body of a girl lying about 200 yards beyond the Little Stretton turn towards Gaulby on the Gartree Road *(Via Devana)* and near a gate leading into a field of mowing grass. Her feet were in the ditch and the rest of her body from her knees upwards was lying on the grass. About six feet from the body, in direct line with it, and on the metal part of the road, was a large pool of blood.

I examined the road and also a lady's bicycle, which I found leaning against a field gate, with an electric torch, but I could not make out anything distinctly. With assistance I removed the body to an empty cottage at Stretton Parva. In the left-hand pocket of *(the)* deceased's skirt I found an empty small leather purse and a lady's handkerchief torn; in the left-hand pocket of her raincoat I found a box of Flag matches. I bicycled to Oadby and reported the case to Sergeant Barrett.

It rained on Saturday night *(according to meteorological records, it was light rain)*. The next day, Sunday, at 6am, I visited the place where the body was found. This was on my own initiative. I noticed a thin stain of blood running parallel with the grass on the left side of the road *(looking towards Leicester)* for a distance of five yards. I think it was caused when Mr Cowell moved the body. I continued my examination until 8am but found nothing further. I went to the cottage and examined the bicycle and found a few spots of blood on the left side pedal.

About 10.30am, I telephoned Superintendent Bowley and informed him of the finding of the body. At 11am, I again went to Little Stretton. About 2pm, I again visited Little Stretton and searched the sides of the road, also the hedges and ditches, and found smears of blood on a gate. At 6pm I again visited the place and after a search of upwards of one hour I found the bullet which I have produced here today. I found it in the centre of the metal part of the road, 17½ feet from the pool of blood in which the body was found lying. The bullet was lying in a hoof mark, to all appearances that of a horse.

I at once went on my bicycle for Dr Williams of Billesdon. I met him on the road and I told him what I had found. He asked me to go back to the cottage and wash the blood from the deceased's face. He said he would follow me on in his car. I returned to Stretton, washed the deceased's face, and found the bullet hole in the deceased's left cheek. *Inquest adjourned.*

Fourth Day: Monday 25 August 1919

Inquest concluded.

Verdict: wilful murder against some person or persons unknown.

Exhibit 6. THE CHIEF INSPECTOR'S REPORT

On Tuesday 29 July 1919, Chief Inspector Albert Hawkins wrote a 23-page report for his bosses at the Metropolitan Police, providing a thorough summary of the incident, its investigation and the evidence collected to date. To avoid repetition with facts already given, I have selected passages from the report to provide an insight into the police investigation and prevailing attitudes of the time. The section headings and comments in brackets are mine.

Hawkins was a stout, humorous man who, legend has it, never forgot a criminal's face or voice. Three months later he would be promoted to superintendent in a famous reorganisation of the Metropolitan Police, becoming one of the so-called Big Four in charge of the Criminal Investigation Department at Scotland Yard.

THE EVIDENCE

A. The Investigation

Apart from the finding of the spent bullet, the hedges on the roads have been cut for miles, but so far no trace of any firearm or anything else in connection with the murder has been found.

With able assistance of the local police we have scoured the whole of Leicestershire. We have interrogated every known relative and personal friend of the deceased, and her family, but not one of them can give any idea of anyone they would consider capable from any cause whatever of taking the life of this girl.

We have kept James Evans in Leicester, whose home it will be remembered is at Maltby, near Rotherham, and he has kept observation at various places in Leicester, particularly at her last place of employment, viz. St Mary's Mills, where some hundreds are employed, but he has failed to see anyone whom he could identify as the man he saw at Gaulby with the deceased on the evening of 5 July. Going back to 2 July *(when the bicycle was taken to Leicester cycle dealer Harry Cox for repairs)*, it is quite clear the wanted man was staying in or around Leicester from that date until 5 July, the day of the murder, yet although enquiries have been made at hotels, inns, lodging houses and so on, and various strong appeals have been made in the London and local press, and circulars giving descriptions of men and bicycles offering a reward for information have been distributed to all police forces in the United Kingdom, so far we have had no useful suggestions from the public as to where the man may have resided on any or all of these dates.

I am strongly of the opinion that if it had not been for the persistent manner in which PC97 Alfred Hall followed up his suspicion that Bella Wright had been foully murdered, the case would have been treated by Dr Williams as one of accidental death.

The case was not certified as one of murder until about 8:40pm on Sunday 6 July, or nearly 24 hours after the body had been found *(technically, murder had not been ascertained, only that Bella had been shot)*. The aid of New Scotland Yard was not sought until the afternoon of Friday 11 July, when the County Police had come to a dead end with their enquiries. In spite of these delays, I venture with every respect to give as an opinion that the enquiry was not very materially affected in so far as bringing about an arrest. I am more than convinced that as far as the local police are concerned they acted with a promptness and a thoroughness that must have brought about, in the ordinary conduct of a case, a satisfactory result had they had a sound clue to work upon.

The moment the cruel deed was perpetrated and the murderer got clear of the scene no connection or material of any sort was left to work upon, and unfortunately the case from that aspect has not altered. There is, at this time of reporting, not a vestige of enquiry that has been left undone.

The County Police have concentrated the whole of their efforts to try to locate the suspected man but so far without success. We have made very many enquiries and interviewed numerous people in London and throughout Leicestershire, but all without result or progress toward tracking the wanted man and so far every valuable point has been exhausted.

B. The Challenge of Demobilisation

Stretton Parva, where the murder was committed, is about seven miles outside Leicester, which has a population of about 280,000 *(other sources state it was nearer 230,000)*. There are about eight fairly large villages around Stretton Parva with an aggregate population of something like 20,000 to 30,000 people.

The description of the suspected murderer is one that tallies with a very fair percentage of men, particularly those recently demobilised. In normal times the local police have a very fair knowledge of who is in their respective areas, but latterly such an influx of men have returned to towns and country villages that it is more difficult to know who are the strangers and who are not. Men being away four or five years naturally have so altered that their identity in many cases is not so easy to establish.

C. Possible Motives for Murder

With regard to the man there is ample evidence and hope that he can be identified by Cox, Evans and Measures, the girl Measures and Mrs Palmer, but at present we have no evidence of anyone seeing the girl after she left with the man at Gaulby, and although there is a very strong inference that the man who had his bicycle repaired by Cox and the man seen at Gaulby are identical, it is certainly not conclusive that he committed the murder.

It is not difficult to define a sound theory for the motive, but it does seem to me to be one of three:

1. That the deceased, who according to medical reports was not a virgin, resented overtures and suggestions made to her by this stranger and in consequence he took her life.
2. She unfortunately made the acquaintance of a madman who shot her for no reason whatsoever.
3. She may have had immoral relations with a man previously and that man may have contracted venereal disease and he may have thought, rightly or wrongly, that he had contracted that disease through his connection with Bella Wright.

The first theory is based on these facts. Deceased was engaged to one Archibald Ward, an assistant stoker on *HMS Diadem* at Portsmouth. His statement has been taken and he says he expected to be demobilised in August next *(1919)* and that there was an arrangement between himself and Bella before he joined in April last *(1918)* that the moment he was free of the navy they would marry, although incidentally the correspondence received by her from him, and by him from her, has been carefully examined but there is no mention of the impending marriage in the letters, neither was it known to the parents or relatives that such a ceremony was contemplated, and maybe knowing that her sweetheart was likely to be demobilised in August, that she was anxious to keep clear of trouble and thus declined and resented immoral suggestions.

Comment

We must not forget that Bella Wright's death occurred over a century ago. For almost all Britons today, even those living in Leicestershire, to travel back to the county in 1919 would be like visiting a foreign land. The differences would not only be noticeable in areas such as technology, communications and transport, but also in cultural values. Today it is staggering that contracting venereal disease could even be thought as a possible motive for murder. I would point out, however, that this was an era before antibiotics, when infections were often serious and even fatal. More pertinently, there was a different moral climate regarding sexual relations, especially for women.

Exhibit 7: TRIAL MINUTES

As there is no extant transcript, the following summary provides a complete schedule of events at the trial. For further details of the important testimony see Chapters Five and Six.

The Trial of Ronald Vivian Light

Venue: The Castle, Leicester.

Date: Wednesday 9 June 1920.

Duration: Three days.

Judge: Mr Justice Thomas Horridge.

Prisoner in the Dock: Ronald Vivian Light, 34 years old.

Counsel for the Crown: Sir Gordon Hewart, Attorney General. Assisted by Mr Henry Maddocks and Mr Norman Birkett.

Counsel for the Prisoner: Sir Edward Marshall Hall. Assisted by Mr George Powers.

Clerk of the Assize: George Bancroft.

Note dates in the testimony refer to 1919, unless stated otherwise.

First Day: Wednesday 9 June 1920

Arraignment

The Clerk of the Assize read the indictment of murder, and asked the defendant how he pleaded.

Light: Not guilty.

The Case for the Crown

The opening speech for the Crown, delivered by the Attorney General Sir Gordon Hewart, outlined the prosecution's case. Counsel summarised the events leading to the discovery of the body. Referring to the verdict of the coroner's inquest, there was no doubt that the young woman had been murdered. Counsel then reviewed subsequent events, and the actions of the prisoner. Although the prisoner's motive for murder was unknown, it was also unnecessary for the prosecution's case. It was suggested, however, that the prisoner had made an unwanted overture to the woman and had been rebuffed. The prisoner shot her. To conceal his involvement in the crime, he disposed of the bicycle and holster, and made false statements. The circumstantial evidence pointed in one direction: to the guilt of the prisoner. If the jury were satisfied that the prisoner had fired the shot, then it must deliver a guilty verdict.

Mr William Keay, county architect and engineer, explained the map exhibits, which showed the principal locations connected with the case. The shortest route from Gaulby to Stoughton, where the deceased lived, and to Leicester, where the accused lived, was by the 'Upper Road' and not the lower road *(Via Devana)* where the body of Bella Wright was found.

Mrs Mary Wright, mother of the deceased, confirmed that, on the evening of Monday 7 July, she had identified a body at Stretton Parva as being that of her eldest child, Annie Bella Wright. She also described the last movements of Bella prior to her fateful cycle ride to Gaulby.

Mr Joseph Cowell, farmer, described how he discovered the body of Bella Wright *{his testimony was the same as given at the inquest – see Exhibit 5}*. Cross-examined by the defence, Cowell estimated the distance from the crime scene to the nearest cottage at Stretton Parva as 220 yards.

In his signed statement to the police, dated 14 July 1919, Cowell said that, prior to discovering the body, he was walking in his fields when he saw "a man and woman each riding a bicycle along the road on which the deceased was found but could not identify either". He also stated that when he first saw the body he was 400 yards distant and he thought it was a yellow horse rug.

Police Constable Alfred Hall, described his arrival at the scene on 5 July, and how he believed, at the time, that the death was not the result of foul play. He told of his discovery of the bullet in the road the following day, which led him to re-examine the body and find a bullet hole near the left eye. Under cross-examination, Hall stated he had first believed that the girl had fallen from her bicycle and died. He also stated that he examined the blood on the field gate, concluding that this was due to a 'raven' which had gorged on the blood near the body and subsequently died.

Miss Muriel Nunney, a 14-year-old girl, was asked by the prosecution whether she had been cycling with a friend on 5 July. The defence objected, claiming the witness was being led by the suggestion of the date *(the judge agreed)*. Muriel identified the prisoner as the man riding a green bicycle who had approached her and a friend. Under cross-examination, the witness said that the date of the encounter with the man had been prompted by the police when she gave her statement.
Adjournment for lunch.

Miss Valeria Caven, a 12-year-old schoolgirl, described how the prisoner approached her and Miss Nunney. He rode a green bicycle, wore a light suit and carried a mackintosh.

Dr Edward Williams explained that on the night of 5 July, between 11pm and 11:30pm, he made a 'casual examination' to establish that the girl was dead. He estimated the time of death to be an hour-and-a-half prior to his arrival, and that its cause was due to an accident. The following day, a more thorough examination revealed the girl had been shot. Under cross-examination, he said that he arrived at the scene between 10:45pm and 11:15pm. He believed the bullet had been fired from close range *(less than 7 feet)*, and also that the clean entrance wound suggested that the bullet had travelled at high velocity.

In his testimony at the committal hearing, Williams

stated he had not been able to identify the minute particles of metal surrounding the entrance wound. He also conceded that the .455 calibre bullet was thicker than an ordinary pencil and bigger than the pencil he had placed into the wound. On cross-examination, he maintained that the wound might have been caused by the .455 bullet (see Chapter 5 for more details).

Mrs Kathleen Powers, employee of the vicarage, Evington, testified that on the afternoon of 5 July she sold the deceased some stamps and posted several letters for her.

Mr Thomas Nourish, farmer, was herding cattle on the upper road towards Gaulby on 5 July between 7pm and 7:30pm. He had observed a man and a woman cycling towards Gaulby. He later saw the same man waiting by the road. He was about 35 years old, wore a grey suit and needed a shave.

Mrs Elizabeth Palmer, of Illston-on-Hill, testified that she saw a man and woman cycle into Gaulby. The girl dismounted and entered Mr Measures' cottage.

Mr George Measures, a roadman, said the deceased was his niece. He identified the prisoner as the cyclist standing outside his house, and who later had spoken to his niece, saying "Bella, you were a long time." Under cross-examination, the witness testified that Bella had told him that she did not know the waiting cyclist.

Mr James Evans, a miner and son-in-law of George Measures, identified the prisoner as the cyclist who had said, "Bella, you have been a long time." He believed that the assembled bicycle shown in court was similar to the prisoner's.

Miss Ethel Tunnicliffe, a friend of the prisoner, told of the occasion *(in summer 1915)* when the prisoner had sent her a parcel, which she then had to deliver to the prisoner's house in Leicester. She was present when the parcel was opened – it contained a revolver.

Mr Frederick Morris, a metal patternmaker, explained that he and the prisoner had shared lodgings when they both worked for Midland Railway in Derby. He recognised the bicycle in court as the one that had been used by the prisoner almost daily.

Second Day: Thursday 10 June 1920
The Case for the Crown (continued)
Police Constable Alfred Hall, (recalled) confirmed details regarding the identification of the body.

Mr Joseph Orton, Derby bicycle dealer, confirmed the prisoner bought bicycle number 103648 and paid for it on 18 May 1910. The only special feature of the bicycle was a back-pedalling rim brake.

Mr Albert Davis, a clerk for Birmingham Small Arms *(BSA)* Company, Redditch, confirmed that on 3 May 1910 it received an order for a green BSA Deluxe gents bicycle from Orton Brothers in Derby.

Mr Sidney Garfield, an employee of BSA Company, Redditch, confirmed that bicycle serial number 103648 was dispatched to Orton Brothers, Derby, in June 1910.

Mr Harry Atkins, a farm labourer, stated that he saw a man and woman cycling on the 'Upper Road' towards Gaulby between 7pm and 7:30pm on 5 July. He heard the man speak in a high tone, but could not discern what he said.

Mrs Mary Webb, employed by Catherine Light, the prisoner's mother, at 54 Highfield Street, Leicester, where the prisoner also lived. She testified that the prisoner cycled daily until 6 July 1919. She recalled that the prisoner went out on his bicycle after tea on 5 July, returning at 10pm looking tired and dusty. She also recalled the bicycle was kept in the house until just before Christmas. She stated the bicycle in the court resembled the one used by the prisoner.

At the committal hearing in March 1920, Webb said that Light "did not return until 10pm. He looked tired and dusty. I asked him why he was late. He said his bicycle had broken down again and he had to walk. The bicycle was put in the back kitchen. It remained there for several days and then it went into the box room at the top of the house. To overhaul it, he said. One night he fetched it down and took it out. He did not bring it back. He told me a week or so afterwards – just before Christmas 1919 – that he had sold it."

Dr Edward Williams (recalled) formally stated that Bella Wright died from a gunshot wound.

Mr Enoch Whitehouse, a canal boatman, observed that on 23 February 1920 his tow rope snagged on a bicycle in the canal. He returned the following day and retrieved a green bicycle from the canal.

Mr Joseph Chambers, a dredger, testified that on 29 to 30 April 1920 he retrieved bicycle components from the canal.

Police Sergeant William Healey, stated that on 19 March 1920 he retrieved a revolver holster and nineteen cartridges from the canal.

Mr Henry Clarke, Leicester gunsmith, said it was a .455 calibre bullet that was discovered in the road by PC Hall. It was adapted for army service smokeless *(cordite)* cartridges. It was an identical type of bullet to that used in the cartridges retrieved from the canal. Under cross-examination, the witness agreed that billions of such bullets had been produced, as it was standard army issue dating from the Boer War. The witness agreed that the bullet could have been fired from a rifle, as well as from a revolver. He also stated that the relatively small exit wound was consistent with the bullet, the size of the exit wound being dependent on the bullet's velocity.

At the committal hearing, Clarke testified that the penetrating power of a bullet is dependent on its velocity, and the velocity would be dependent on the quality of the firearm. He also stated that if the bullet were discharged within four yards *(12ft)* he would expect to find blackening of the skin on the deceased. He believed the marks on the bullet had been caused when it hit a hard substance, possibly ricocheting after passing through the deceased's skull. Some of the marks could have been caused by a horse treading on the bullet when it was lying on the road.

Mr Walter Franks, bicycle dealer, Leicester, stated that in the spring of 1919 he had repaired the green BSA bicycle of the prisoner, fitting black mudguards.
Adjournment for lunch.

Mr Harry Cox, bicycle dealer, Leicester, testified that the prisoner entered his premises on Wednesday 2 July, and asked for his three-speed gear to be adjusted. He told the witness that he had been an army officer, was on a month's leave and was visiting Leicester to see friends. Prisoner returned on Friday 4 July to have the gear cable shortened. The prisoner was wearing a raincoat and badly needed a shave.

Mr William Saunders, cycle shop manager, stated that on 1 March 1920 he had found the serial number 103648 on the front fork of the green bicycle frame. The usual place for a serial number (on the seat pillar plug) had been filed away.

Police Superintendent Levi Bowley said the first police handbill, offering a reward and description of both the man and the green bicycle, was circulated in mainland

Britain on 8 July.

Detective Superintendent Herbert Taylor interviewed the prisoner at a Cheltenham college on 4 March 1920. The prisoner denied owning a green bicycle, later admitting he had owned one but had sold it to a Mr Bourne of Derby. He was taken back to Cheltenham police station for further questioning and was later charged.

Police Detective Sergeant Harold Illes confirmed that the prisoner was identified by Henry Cox as the owner of the green BSA bicycle who had visited his cycle shop in the days before the death of Bella Wright.

Mr Henry Clarke (recalled) stated that Bella's wounds were not self-inflicted.
This concluded the case for the Crown.

The Case for the Defence
The opening speech for the Defence was short. Marshall Hall said simply: "My Lord, I desire to call the prisoner."

Mr Ronald Light stated that he first owned a revolver in July 1915. He bought a Webley & Scott service revolver from his commanding officer. The prisoner confirmed that the green bicycle and the holster exhibits in court were his. He explained he was sent to casualty clearing in August 1918 for "shellshock and deafness" and that he had been slightly deaf ever since. He had not seen his revolver since he left France.

He denied meeting the two schoolgirls. He denied knowing Bella Wright, but confirmed that he had met her on the 'Upper Road' on the evening she died. They cycled together to Gaulby, and the prisoner waited for the girl because she had said to him, "I shall only be 10 minutes," which he interpreted as meaning she wanted to continue the ride. He denied knowing her name until he read newspaper reports of her death. When she emerged from the cottage, the prisoner had said, "Hello, you've been a long time," and denied calling her Bella.

The girl turned left shortly after leaving Gaulby. The prisoner continued on the 'Upper Road', and arrived home at a little before 10pm. He first heard of her death by reading the *Leicester Mercury* on Tuesday 8 July. He admitted he had thrown the bicycle into the canal after loosening some parts.

Under cross-examination by the prosecution, the prisoner admitted filing off the serial number from his bicycle. He had told his mother that he had sold the bicycle. The prisoner denied he had ever met the schoolgirls – they had been mistaken, he claimed.

Third Day: Friday 11 June 1920
The Case for the Defence (continued)

The cross-examination of the defendant resumed. The prisoner stated that he and the deceased arrived at Gaulby between 7:15pm and 7:30pm. They left the village at about 8:40pm. His bicycle had a slight puncture and the homeward journey took longer than normal. He saw a story about the death in the *Leicester Mercury*, and realised he was the man on the green bicycle and wanted for questioning by the police. He did not come forward because he was "dazed about the whole thing" and was not thinking clearly. "Everyone had jumped to the conclusion that the man with the green bicycle had murdered the girl." He stated that failing to come forward was a mistake, but it had not been a deliberate decision – due to fright, he had "drifted into doing nothing at all". Further, if he had come forward, he did not think that he would have been believed. He amended this last point, saying he thought he would have been believed, but feared "unpleasant publicity". Further, he could give no information as to the cause of death. He now appreciated that the police would have eliminated him from its enquiries and this would have been helpful.

He told the court that the raincoat and other clothes he had been wearing on 5 July were sold to Mrs Ridgeway, a 'wardrobe dealer' in Leicester. He admitted he hid his green bicycle in his house to prevent it being identified. He filed off the serial number for the same reason.
Adjournment for lunch.

Re-examined by the Defence, the prisoner told of his family, and also that he had "not been the same" after suffering shellshock in the Great War. He had sold his raincoat at Christmas when his mother was selling many items, because it was his oldest coat.

Mr Keay (recalled) confirmed that the lower road *(Via Devana)* was the longer route for the prisoner to return home from Gaulby, and that the dead body was found one mile 300 yards from the gated junction where Ronald

Light said he had parted from Bella Wright. *(Note: It was also the longer route for Bella Wright to have returned home, by a similar distance).*

The Closing Speeches

The closing speech for the Crown, by Mr Maddocks, began by telling the jury that there was no doubt that Bella Wright had been murdered. He dismissed the possibility of an accident. The question was: who fired the shot? The prisoner had been with the girl 35 minutes before her body was found, and he had repeatedly concealed his involvement. Not only had the prisoner engaged in suspicious behaviour and remained silent, he had also lied. He told the police he had never owned a green bicycle. Had he come forward earlier, more enquiries could have been made to verify his story, to show his innocence, as he claimed. The opportunity had been lost.

The prisoner had remained silent for a wrong motive, had told untruths for a wrong motive and had disposed of the evidence for a wrong motive, Counsel said. He then reviewed the evidence for the jury, stressing that Measures and Evans had heard the prisoner address the victim as "Bella", implying that he knew the girl. And after waiting all this time for her, would he have let her part so easily?

The girl had been shot dead using a heavy revolver cartridge. The bullet that killed her was of a special kind – made for use with black powder and adapted for use with cordite. The same bullets were owned by the prisoner. What an unfortunate coincidence for the prisoner!

The prisoner had returned home with a puncture, yet

neglected to have it repaired on the Sunday, Monday or Tuesday, before the news was made public that a green bicycle was connected to the case. Was he already preparing his defence? He said he was dazed by the news. Why? His actions had been those of a guilty man, anxious to cover up his tracks and dissociate himself from the green bicycle. Could the jury accept the prisoner's word?

The closing speech for the Defence, by Sir Edward Marshall Hall, reminded the jury that a life was at stake, and that the jury had to be satisfied beyond a reasonable doubt that the prisoner had killed Bella Wright. First, they had to be satisfied the girl was murdered. The prosecution had tried to make out that Light had concealed his identity to the cycle dealer Cox days before, as if Light had made up his mind deliberately to meet and kill Bella Wright. But what had the deceased said to her uncle? The prisoner had been a perfect stranger to her.

None of the witnesses who claimed to have seen Light that evening mentioned seeing a revolver or even something weighty in one of his coat pockets. Marshall Hall asserted that the wound produced could not have been made by the bullet found in the road. He criticised the doctor for not handing over his gruesome exhibit *(the preserved cheek skin)* for expert analysis to ascertain whether it was made by a .455 calibre bullet.

There was absolutely no sign of motive. There was no witness claiming to have seen the prisoner and the deceased cycling together after leaving Gaulby, and no witness to say that they even knew each other. The prisoner had showed moral cowardice, but this might be accounted for by his shellshock and because he did not want to alarm his mother. He did not hide the bicycle immediately, but kept it in the kitchen for 10 days in plain sight.

The two-hour speech closed as it had begun. Marshall Hall stated this was a matter of life and death, and unless the evidence left no doubt, the presumption of innocence applied. *Adjournment.*

The Summing Up

The judge's charge to the jury, given by Mr Justice Horridge, stressed the prosecution had to prove beyond reasonable doubt that the prisoner was guilty. This burden would not be met if the jury merely disbelieved the prisoner's story. If the prisoner had put up a story that the jury believed was untrue, this was a factor to be considered in deciding the question.

The judge read through the evidence of George Measures, and that the girl had said the prisoner was a perfect stranger to her. He turned his attention to the deception and asked whether it would have been practised by an innocent man or a guilty one. The jury had to consider all the circumstances under which they met and how long the prisoner had waited, and ask whether they would have parted in the way he said they had.

He advised the jury to ignore two minor points: the statements of the schoolgirls and the allegation that the prisoner made a false statement to the cycle dealer Cox. He further advised that the jury needed to look closely at a case in which there was no apparent motive. If they were satisfied the evidence pointed to guilt, motive was irrelevant.

If they were not satisfied, motive was an important factor, yet no motive had been suggested by the prosecution.

Did the prisoner own a revolver which could have fired the bullet? If there was doubt, the jury should also consider the fact that there was no motive.

The Verdict

After three hours of deliberation by the jury, the foreman of the jury announced its verdict. The prisoner was found not guilty.

Exhibit 8: ABSENT WITNESSES

For various reasons, four potential witnesses did not take the stand at the trial. Their evidence is now being placed before the Cold Case Jury.

Robert Churchill, ballistics expert

One mistake in the prosecution of the case was to place the ballistics evidence in the hands of Henry Clarke, a local gunsmith, instead of approaching Robert Churchill, a renowned expert at the time. If Churchill had been called as an expert witness the jury's verdict might have been very different.

Marshall Hall seized the opportunity presented by the prosecution's mistake and approached Churchill, asking him to appear for the defence and rebut the claims of Clarke. But Churchill's report for Hall must have left the Great Defender a little shaken. In it, Churchill believed the bullet found by PC Alfred Hall was fired from a revolver and not a rifle. Further, by examining the grooves and twists, the bullet could have only been fired by a Webley & Scott and no other make of weapon.

This was sensational evidence that would have sunk Marshall Hall's defence. But what of Marshall Hall's claim that such a bullet fired from short distance would inflict far more serious injuries than those sustained by Bella? Churchill stated that fired at such close range the bullet did not have sufficient time to reach maximum velocity. Such a view would not be supported by ballistics experts today, but on the stand it would have refuted the defence's position and possibly sent Ronald Light to the gallows. So who is right on this point? It depends. If the revolver and bullet were in good condition, it appears Marshall Hall would be on the stronger ground. On the other hand, if the barrel of the gun or the ammunition was corroded then the gun might not fire with its usual power, the bullet 'fizzing off'. The answer was in the revolver. Despite intensive efforts by the police, the failure to trace the gun was the evidential weak link in the case.

Alfred Johnson, tenant farmer

In his unpublished memoir, PC Alfred Hall claims that one Sunday after the committal hearing, which ended on 24 March 1920, farmer Alfred Johnson visited him brandishing a newspaper. Johnson was adamant that he and his fiancée, May Walker, recognised Ronald Light, who was pictured in that day's edition of the *News of the World*. They saw him on the road between Stretton Parva and Great Glen on 5 July 1919 at about 9:15pm (see Chapter 8).

Although other late witnesses, such as the two

schoolgirls, were called to the stand, Johnson and his fiancée were not. Hall writes that his superiors believed Johnson's testimony was "quite useless". It should be borne in mind that Light had reserved his defence and had not given a statement detailing his movements. Perhaps the police only realised the significance of Johnson's evidence when Light stepped into the witness box and told his story for the first time – particularly, he did not travel home via Great Glen. If so, we can only imagine their dismay at discovering the mistake.

There is no mention of Johnson's statement anywhere except in Hall's memoir. Can it be trusted? I have examined the memoir in detail and discovered an astonishing number of discrepancies between it and facts asserted under oath at the time, including Hall's own testimony. For example, the memoir states the following:

✢ Cowell was with his daughter, Marion, when the body was found

✢ At the coroner's inquest, Cowell stated that Marion fixed the time of the body's discovery at 9:20pm by looking at her wristwatch

✢ Hall travelled in Cowell's float from Great Glen to the scene of Bella's death

✢ Hall telephoned Dr Williams to come to the scene

✢ When Hall arrived, the bicycle was on top of the body

✢ The body had not been moved since its discovery

There are other discrepancies, but taking these six in turn:

✢ Cowell never testified that his daughter was with him

✢ Cowell told the inquest that he looked at *his* watch

✢ Hall said that he cycled to the scene

✣ According to both Cowell and Dr Williams, Cowell telephoned Dr Williams
✣ When Hall arrived, the bicycle was leaning against the field gate
✣ Cowell told Hall that the body had been moved

All of the above can be confirmed by reading the inquest testimony of Hall, Cowell and Williams in Exhibit 5. In addition, in his memoir, Hall says he found the dead crow on the morning of Sunday 6 July and immediately opened it up at Cowell's farmhouse. Yet, according to Chief Inspector Hawkins of Scotland Yard, Superintendent Taylor examined the dead crow on Monday 7 July when it was known Bella Wright had been shot. The relevant section from the report is reproduced in Chapter 7.

Most of these details could be gleaned by anyone looking at the newspaper accounts of the trial, so it is difficult to believe that someone so intimately involved in the case should misremember so many. Although it is not known when Hall wrote his memoir, a covering letter found with the document shows his handwritten notes (now lost) were typed up in 1957. If Hall's recollections were written almost 40 years after the event, the most charitable explanation is that his memory was fading by this time. A less charitable interpretation is that Hall was self-aggrandising in his memoir. Perhaps it was a combination of both.

If the Hall Memoir contains inaccuracies, where does this leave Alfred Johnson's alleged sighting of Light? Is it reliable? There are two pieces of circumstantial evidence that point to its truth. Although there is no police record of Johnson's statement, the Bowley Statement mentions Light encountering "courting couples" on Stretton Road. The statement and the memoir are consistent on this point. Further, genealogical records show that Alfred Johnson married Gertrude May Walker in the summer of 1926. The memoir accurately states May's age and the name of her father. There can be no doubting they were a couple living in the vicinity of Great Glen at the time. I attempted to trace their living grandchildren to see if they knew of the story but without success.

Against this, the following must be weighed. There was no photograph of Ronald Light in the *News of the World* before the trial. On 7 March 1920, Light's arrest is reported in the national newspaper (see note 1, end of section). A longer article regarding Light's committal for trial appeared three weeks later (see note 2, end of section). Neither carried any photograph. After the trial, on 13 June, a story on the verdict was accompanied by a photograph of Light leaning forward in the dock, his chin resting on his hands (3). It is hardly a clear image of his face, although it does show his large nose.

It is possible that Light's photograph was in a different paper but, yet again, Hall's memoir contains an incorrect detail. It is for the Cold Case Jury to decide how much weight to place upon this evidence. Johnson's testimony, if accepted, shows that Light lied and places him near to the scene of Bella's death.

Agnes Olive Measures, Bella's cousin

Agnes Measures, a 12-year-old schoolgirl, was not called to give evidence at either the inquest or the trial. It was probably believed her testimony added little to the case so she could be spared the ordeal of testifying. However, her testimony provides further insight into the question of whether Light and Bella knew each other. Below is her verbatim police statement:

"On the 5th July I saw my cousin, Bella, at about 8:45pm. She was getting ready to go home. I saw her with a spanner in her hand. I saw a man outside the gate holding his bicycle, talking to Jim *(James Evans)*. I heard the man say, 'This *(is)* rather a heavy machine,' that was when he was lifting his own machine.

"While Jim was tightening up Bella's bicycle, I saw the man whisper something to Bella and they both laughed. He then said to Bella, 'I think I'll put my coat on,' which he did. I then saw both the man and Bella leave together, going in the direction of the Leicester road. Bella said 'goodnight' but the man did not speak or say 'goodnight' to me.

"I should know the man. He had rather a pointed-looking nose. He had a green-coloured bicycle with black mudguards. I heard him say that he had had his bicycle mended."

Margaret Louisa Evans, Bella's cousin.

Margaret Evans was the 22-year-old daughter of George Measures and the wife of James Evans. She had given testimony at the coroner's inquest but was not called to give evidence at the trial, probably because she failed to identify Ronald Light at a line-up. Her police statement provides more details about Bella's final two hours:

"Annie Bella Wright is my cousin. She came over to see

us on Saturday 5th July at about 7 o'clock. She came over on my bicycle *(this seems unlikely)*. About half an hour after Bella's arrival, I came downstairs. I had not seen her since I was 14 years of age. She was nursing my youngest baby when I came downstairs and was very cheerful.

"About 8pm my father went to the door and looked out. It was broad daylight. My father said, 'Is that man out there waiting for you, Bella?' She said, 'What man, I have not a man waiting for me.' Father said, 'There is a man out there with a bicycle *(who)* looks old enough to be your father.' My husband, James Evans, who was present said, 'Yes, there is a man up there waiting with a bicycle.'

"Bella said, 'I wonder whether it is the man who overtook me coming along on the way, who said he had come from Great Glen'… My husband and also my father said, 'It looks as though he is waiting for you. He keeps on walking up and down.' Bella said, 'I'll stop a bit longer and see if he goes.' She did not at any time get up from her chair to see who this man was. She stayed for about another quarter of an hour when she then got up to go and we all got to the door to see her off.

"Bella's freewheel was not quite right and my husband adjusted it for her. As soon as she got hold of her bike the man came down the road with his bike and said to Bella, 'You have been a long time. I thought you had gone another way.' She did not answer but went very red and confused. We thought at first that he was a complete stranger but afterwards thought by the way they went away *(there was)* a sort of familiarity between them, that they were not complete strangers…

"I said, 'Do you really know who that man is, Bella?' She said, 'No, he is the one who has overtaken me on the road.' Father said in my presence, 'I should make haste home, Bella, I don't like the look of him.' She said, 'Yes, I will. I shall be able to go on in front of him on my bicycle.'

"Bella and the man left about 8:30 or 8:45pm, pushing their respective bicycles. She spoke to him but I did not hear what she said as I was in the kitchen. They went away quite friendly."

Notes
(1) 'Murder of Pretty Girl', the *News of the World*, 7 March 1920. As an aside, this article states Ronald Light was 5' 5" tall
(2) 'Green Bicycle Mystery', the *News of the World*, 28 March 1920
(3) 'Schoolmaster Freed', the *News of the World*, 13 June 1920

Exhibit 9: THE BOWLEY STATEMENT
Below is the full statement of Levi Bowley, signed three days after the acquittal of Ronald Light. I am grateful to Simon Cole, Chief Constable of Leicestershire Police, for granting permission to publish it.

I have reproduced the text of the document faithfully, including any grammatical and punctuation errors. I have included paragraph breaks missing from the original to make it easier to read.

County Police Station, Leicester.
14th June, 1920.
At about 11 am this day RONALD VIVIAN LIGHT (who

was on 11th instant acquitted of the Murder of ANNIE
BELLA WRIGHT, at Stretton Parva, on 5th July, 1919)
came to this Office to arrange for his property to be
handed back to him. I talked with him for about an
hour-and-a-quarter about his Trial and about the Murder
generally. He and I were together in my Office with the
door closed. I pointed out amongst other things that I could
not swallow his story of his leaving the girl where and how
he said he had done, knowing as I did, of his fondness for
women and his past history in this respect. I returned to
this subject time after time and told him that I did not
believe he had wilfully shot her and that I never had
believed that of him.

When Light was in my custody I had endeavoured to
make him as comfortable as was possible, and had allowed
him certain privileges which he missed when on remand at
Prison. In consequence of this he was on good terms with
me and said, "Well, you are a good Sport, if I tell you
something can I depend upon your keeping it to yourself?" I
said, Yes, strictly. He said,– "Well I'll tell you, but mind it
must be strictly confidential, no other person knows it and if
you divulge it I shall, of course, say I never told you anything
of the kind. He went on to say – I did shoot the girl but it was
completely accidental, we were riding quietly along, I was
telling her about the War and my experiences in France, I
had my Revolver in my Raincoat pocket and we dismounted
for her to look at it. I had fired off some shots in the
afternoon for practice and I had no idea there was a loaded
cartridge in it, we were both standing by the sides of our
bicycles, I think she had dismounted on the right of her

machine and that the two bicycles were between us. I took the Revolver from my Coat pocket and was in the act of handing it to her, I am not sure whether she actually took hold of it or not, but her hand was out to take it when it went off. She fell and never stirred, I was horror struck, I did not know what to do, I knew she was dead, I did not touch her.

I was frightened and altogether unnerved and I got on my bicycle and rode away, I went by Great Glen, I saw some courting couples between Stretton and Glen and I slowed down somewhat so that I should not be unduly noticed, I thought that as no one knew me I should get clear away, and as time went on I thought it would never be found out. I cannot account for the shot unless it was that the Revolver was fully cocked, the least touch would fire it then. Mary Webb's evidence was quite true, and whenever the subject of the Murder was brought up I always said as little as possible and commenced to talk of something else.

I did not know the girl, I had never met her before that evening. What I said about her asking me for a Spanner was quite true, I first saw her at the top of the hill, I screwed her bicycle up and we went down the hill then started to go up the next hill where Atkins saw us. I did not make any improper suggestion to her either on the way to Gaulby or after leaving there. I did not mention that at all, that might – and probably would, have happened later. If I had intended shooting her I should never have done it close up to the village, it was much more lonely along the road we had passed. I do not remember the two little girls, they must have mistaken me for someone else.

I asked Light about the bullet – He said – I do not

believe that the bullet found in the road is the one which was shot by the Revolver as it would have travelled much further, and from the position in which we were standing it could not have struck the ground, and if it had struck a tree it would have buried itself in the tree, and besides it would not have been found at that angle.

It was, I think, in October that I threw the bicycle in the Canal. I unscrewed everything as far as I could before leaving home, I then walked with the machine to the Canal and got on the towing-path at Walnut Street Bridge, it would be about 10 o'clock when I got there. I first threw in the mudguards, then the gearcase, then the chain, then the Cranks & pedals and so on until I had thrown it all in, the holster was full of cartridges to sink it. I said– If you had left the Revolver in the holster that would have kept it down– Is that in there too? He said– No, I had it with me and it was loaded. I was in such a nervous state that if anyone had interfered with me I should have been guilty of murder, I should have shot him. I remember a man passing me as soon as I had got on the towing path, I pretended to be doing something at my bicycle and he did not speak to me. I said– Where is the Revolver? He replied– It is in the Canal but not there, I threw that and another in near to Belgrave Gate.

I said Did your Counsel know All this?" He said No, I told Mr. Powers I was not at Gaulby at all, and it was not until later that I was persuaded to tell them part of the truth. I told them the story I told in Court. I was asked about it being an accident but I adhered to the story that I left the girl at the two roads. I dared not admit the shot, I was afraid of a verdict of Manslaughter. I said You ran a great risk. He said— I suppose I did but I would rather have my neck stretched than do 10 years in prison. I asked Light to give permission to tell the Chief Constable what he had told me. He declined to do so but eventually, after much pressing, he said— You can do so after a while but not at present. I said— Does your Mother know? He said My God no, I would not let my mother know it for the world. No one on this earth knows it but us two, and if you tell I shall say I never said anything of the kind.

L. Bowley (signed) Superintendent.

Exhibit 10: THE HOLMES COMMUNIQUÉS

On Wednesday 23 June 1920, just nine days after the Bowley Statement was written, a letter was sent to Chief Constable Holmes from the Director of Public Prosecutions (DPP). It reveals that a confidential document was being discussed with a view to instigating a perjury prosecution. The fact that the DPP wished to discuss the matter in person with Holmes or Bowley shows how sensitive the matter was.

Members of the Cold Case Jury, is this letter clear evidence that the Bowley Statement was being taken seriously with a view to prosecuting Ronald Light? If so, it confirms the authenticity of the statement.

... Letter Begins ...
Confidential
1 Richmond Terrace
23 June 1920
Sir,

Re: Light
Referring to your call yesterday, and to the document you
left with me, I beg to say that we have been in consultation
with the Attorney General as to what use, if any, should be
made of the information contained in that document, and
that he has decided that a prosecution for perjury should be
instituted if the necessary evidence is forthcoming.

In these circumstances, and for reasons which you will
appreciate, I think it desirable that such suggestions as I
have to make in the matter should be made verbally either
to yourself, or to Superintendent Bowley, and I shall be
glad if one or the other of you can make it convenient to
attend here for this purpose, say, on Friday next, the 25th
instant, at about 12 noon. I shall be glad to know by wire if
I may expect you.

Yours obediently,
... *Letter Ends* ...

At 11:16am on Thursday 24 June, a telegram was sent
stating that Holmes hoped to attend the next day at noon,
as suggested in the letter.

After further communication, the DPP wrote to Holmes
in a letter dated 19 July 1920, referenced "Rex v. Light". It
stated that "the course of procedure which has been
discussed between us appears to be impossible. The matter,
therefore, must remain where it is unless any further, or
precise, information should come to light as to the
whereabouts of the weapon." He added that the matter
"has been laid before the Attorney General who quite
agrees with *(this)* view". No prosecution for perjury was

undertaken.

The final letter raises the fascinating possibility that Leicestershire Constabulary might have considered locating the revolvers in the canal. As stated earlier, the retrieval of the revolvers in a place close to where Light said he dumped them would be additional evidence for the accuracy of the Bowley Statement.

PART THREE

The Verdict

You have read the story.
You have sifted the evidence.
How was Bella Wright killed?
Here is my judgement.

One cool judgment is worth a thousand hasty counsels.

Woodrow Wilson, President of the United States
(1913 – 1921)

MY JUDGEMENT

How was Bella Wright killed? There are three possible verdicts in this case.

Misadventure. Bella Wright was shot accidentally by a person unknown

Manslaughter. Bella Wright was shot unintentionally by Ronald Light

Murder. Bella Wright was wilfully killed by Ronald Light

In the summing up I asked three questions. Now I will provide my answers for each. The first was Do you believe that Ronald Light was involved in the killing of Bella Wright? The short answer is yes. First, we must eliminate the 'shooting crows' theory. There is no doubt that this theory adds much colour and fascination to the case, but I cannot accept it as a plausible explanation as to how Bella died. The most damning objection is that there simply is no evidence that the crow was shot. The old adage "absence of evidence is not evidence of absence" does not apply here because the police examined the dead crow for a gunshot wound and found none. It is simply not credible to suggest that a rifle can fatally injure a bird without leaving obvious wounds. Indeed, had the crow been hit by a large-calibre bullet it would have been found in pieces by the wooden gate.

It is important to recall the exact words in the report of Chief Inspector Hawkins: the bird's crop, or gullet, was full of new blood. Without an obvious head or neck wound, this strongly suggests the crow had ingested it. The police concluded that the crow had choked to death, probably after gorging on the blood on the road after the body had been removed. It is a ghoulish thought but this is the best explanation for its cameo appearance in our story. The probable presence of stippling on Bella's cheek suggests the weapon was fired from close range, again counting against the 'shooting crows' theory.

I also believe the Bowley Statement to be authentic beyond a reasonable doubt. Based on the forensic and content analysis and the existence of the Holmes Communiqués, I am convinced that the conversation took place as the superintendent reported it. It is difficult to believe Light would lie about his involvement if he was totally innocent, and hence I believe the 'shooting crows' theory is false.

With respect to the statement, I believe Chief Constable Edward Holmes took the most reasonable course of action available to him. Given its sensitive nature but historical importance, he locked it away knowing that one day its contents would become publicly known, and that future generations would infer that he and his officers believed Light was culpable for the death of Bella Wright.

So step forward, Ronald Light. But was it murder or manslaughter? This largely turns on your view of the confessional statement. Even if the account was accurately recorded by Bowley, did Light finally tell the truth? He stated that he did not meet the two schoolgirls, but I believe it far more likely that he, rather than the girls, is lying. Further, it is hard to think they would make a mistake in identifying him. How many instances of an unshaven man riding on a green bicycle carrying a mackintosh over his shoulder could there be? Remember, Light had a history of this sort of thing.

I also believe – largely based on the testimony of Bella's cousin Margaret Evans and her husband Jim – that there was a familiarity between Ronald Light and Bella. It was obviously not a close friendship, more of an acquaintance-ship, but one in which Light called her by her first name. Of course, this does not imply that the familiarity was welcomed by Bella. The relationship might have been that of a nuisance stalker and his victim. So, Did Ronald Light know Bella Wright? My answer is yes.

In my opinion, Ronald Light lied to Bowley during the confessional conversation. Nevertheless, it is possible – but only just – that Light might have lied on these points for whatever reason and then told the truth about what transpired with the shooting. The problem is that Light's account of the accident is vague. Although Bowley might not have pushed him on the details, it is unclear exactly what happened. In particular, how could Bella have sustained her injuries?

Remember the entrance wound was one inch behind her left eye and the bullet travelled from left to right. If you place a finger on your face in that position you will realise it is not possible to be looking at the revolver when it discharged. To make sense of the wounds, I believe she was looking away when the firearm went off. All we glean from Light is that Bella's hand was outstretched and the revolver might have been fully cocked.

All this bears heavily on the third question, What do you make of the explanatory gaps in the confessional statement? They are suspicious, in my view. In particular, I believe the reason that Bella Wright was on the Via Devana, taking a longer route home on a lonely road, was to avoid cycling with Light. This suggests that Ronald Light deliberately followed her. Although I believe much of his confessional account to be true, I do not find the description of the accidental firing plausible, especially as I also believe that he lied about meeting the schoolgirls and knowing Bella. In my opinion, Light lied on all the critical issues connected to his guilt.

On the other hand, I have difficulty in understanding why Light would have shot Bella, even if he had assaulted her. It appears out of character, a crime without motive, and that is why the death of Bella Wright remains a mystery. Maybe there was more to the relationship between them and this led to a more heated altercation. In addition, we must remember that Light had recently returned from the carnage of war in which death was part of the daily routine and life was devalued to the point where the act of killing was almost a conditioned reflex. Did this affect his attitude and behaviour that night? We can only speculate.

The lack of motive strengthens the case for manslaughter, but a lack of motive is insufficient to overturn the evidence that points to one verdict:

Bella Wright was murdered by Ronald Light.

Had I been a juror in 1920, would I have delivered a guilty verdict? No. The prosecution had not shown that he was guilty beyond a reasonable doubt. Light had been crafty in covering his tracks but all the breaks in the case seemed to go in his favour. In particular, he was lucky that some witnesses did not come forward sooner, and that he was able to rely on the services of the Great Defender.

Mark Twain said that the best thing that can befall a person is to be born lucky. With luck, you are always in the right place at the right time. You never have to push against the grain of fate. Things always fall right for you.

With luck, you can even get away with murder.

OTHER VERDICTS

The following brief overview provides my thoughts on the major books and articles published on the case, listed in chronological order. All were sources in writing *The Green Bicycle Mystery*. Where appropriate, the conclusion the author reached is stated.

Humphries, Trueman. *The Green Bicycle Case (1922)*
Although fictionalised, this account published in *The Strand Magazine* proposes a serious solution to the case and has been highly influential with writers. The police had not grasped the significance of the dead crow, Humphries believed. The main premise of his argument is that no crow is known to gorge on human blood, and certainly not in the short time it had available. Rather, the crow was shot as it perched on the field gate. The problem with this theory is that the police claimed to have examined the crow and found no evidence of a gunshot.
Conclusion: Misadventure – Bella Wright was shot

accidentally by a rifleman aiming at a crow.

Villiers, Elizabeth. *The Mystery of the Green Bicycle (1928)*
This is one of 14 short accounts from her book, *The Riddles of Crime*. This particular one is moralistic in tone, Villiers keen to emphasise the maxim that an innocent person should always tell the whole truth immediately. Of course, this assumes that Ronald Light was innocent. She portrays Light sympathetically as a patriotic young man suffering from shellshock who lost his nerve. She also bemoans the fact that the police did not examine the dead crow, one of several errors in her account.
Conclusion: Misadventure – Bella Wright was shot accidentally by a rifleman aiming at a crow.

Wakefield, H Russell. *The Green Bicycle Case (1930)*
The first book published on the case largely deals with the trial. Despite looking for a trial transcript, the author found none. Indeed, there is doubt as to whether an official transcript was ever taken. The trial is reconstructed from contemporaneous newspaper accounts. Sixty years later, Wendy East would provide greater detail about the trial and the background to the case. Nevertheless, there is an excellent summary of the case in the introduction, in which the author propounds his views. Dismissing the crow shooting theory, he believes Bella Wright was shot while she was lying on the ground. The bullet found in the road was the one that killed her, but the person who fired it will forever remain a mystery.
Conclusion: Murder – by person or persons unknown.

OTHER VERDICTS

Marjoribanks, Edward. *Famous Trials of Marshall Hall (1950)*
Sir Edward Marshall Hall, one of the finest-ever English barristers, regarded the Green Bicycle Case as his finest triumph. Fifteen pages of this book cover the trial, and it provides a glimpse of how Marshall Hall approached the case and the problems he faced. The lack of motive, he thought, was a substantial weakness in the prosecution case. Marshall Hall believed his client innocent, and that the bullet found in the road by his namesake was a sheer coincidence. He was said to be amused by the crow-shooting theory.
Conclusion: Ronald Light was innocent.

Rowland, John. *The Green Bicycle Case (1963)*
Rowland's book *Murder Mistaken* has two parts: the first examines the case of Robert Wood, the second explores that of Ronald Light. Rowland compares the stark similarities between the two, claiming that in each case the "young men acted foolishly and both found themselves nearing the scaffold". Like Villiers, he believes the moral is to go to the police and tell the whole truth. He rejects the suggestion that Bella Wright was killed at close range, and suggests a long-range rifle shot was a possibility.
Conclusion: Most likely an accident.

Pearson, Edmund. *The Death of Bella Wright (1964)*
Pearson's article is no more than an overview of the case. He comments that Trueman Humphries' account (see

The Green Bicycle Mystery

above) was worthy of the great Sherlock Holmes. He writes that there are two schools of thought about the crow: the practical, who think it has no connection to the case, and the romantic, who think it is intimately involved. He thought it was "a beautiful case of circumstantial evidence", but that Light could not be shaken or disproved on any detail.
Conclusion: Unsolved, possibly an accident.

Hastings, Macdonald. *The Other Mr Churchill (1966)*
This is the biography of Robert Churchill, who was instrumental in developing forensic ballistics. As it was not a case in which he testified, only five pages are devoted to the Green Bicycle Case, yet it is a fascinating read. Churchill believed that Bella Wright was shot, possibly by accident, by someone waving a gun about to intimidate her. The dead crow, he believed, had been shot but was unconnected to the case. He refused on principle to support Marshall Hall's plea, and was critical of Henry Clarke's view that the bullet found by PC Hall could have been fired from a rifle.
Conclusion: Bella Wright was shot at close range by a Webley & Scott revolver.

East, C. Wendy. *The Green Bicycle Murder (1993)*
The most thorough book on the case. East documents Bella's life and uncovers the details about Light's unsavoury past – his penchant for girls, his War Office deception and his difficulty in holding down a job. She explores the ballistics evidence (as much as there is), concluding that a smaller calibre bullet was probably fired, and suggests the sub-calibre adaption to the Webley & Scott as a likely candidate for the

247

murder weapon. The only evidence East does not examine is the Bowley Statement, which was hidden away in the police archives at the time.

Conclusion: Murder – Light was guilty.

Arthur, Max. *Last Post (2005)* and *We Will Remember Them (2009)*

Both of these books are interviews of World War I veterans, who retold their war experiences and the changes in society they had witnessed during their lifetimes. The second book is more focused, examining the experiences and views of the veterans when they returned home.

Hanson, Neil. *The Unknown Soldier (2005)*

It is an amazing fact: of the million British fatalities during World War I, only one – the Unknown Soldier – was repatriated. In this book, Hanson follows the fortunes of three soldiers, using their own words written in diaries and letters home, and tells the story of the Unknown Soldier. In researching Light's possible war experiences, I drew on this book (and Max Arthur's) to find out what the troops had said about the war.

Donahue, Bill. *The Green Bicycle Murder (Bicycling, December 2007)*

This is a significant article on the case because it is the first to mention the Bowley Statement. To my knowledge, *The Green Bicycle Mystery* is the first to carry the full text. The article is journalistic in tone, with Donahue interviewing experts and other authors to provide insight and background to the events on the Via Devana.

Keay, Alison M. *The Green Bicycle Murder and New Evidence (2010)*
This small volume recounts the case based on the major published works, notably Russell Wakefield and Wendy East, and highlights discrepancies between them, especially over the times of key events. Its main assertion is that the ballistic evidence does not support the view that Bella Wright was shot by a .455 calibre bullet. This is hardly revelatory because it was the main contention of Marshall Hall at the trial. No conclusion is offered.

Research Sources
In researching this book I have relied heavily on primary sources – police reports, witness statements and prosecution files – held at The National Archive (ref: DPP 1/61). The Bowley Statement is held at Leicestershire Records Office.

Epilogue

LIVES MORE ORDINARY

Mary Webb, the housemaid, must have harboured suspicions about Ronald Light. She knew he kept a green bicycle at home and used to cycle daily but stopped suddenly after Bella's death. Yet she said nothing, fearing that if she came forward she would be sacked by her employer, his doting mother. So one might argue that it was not just Light who showed moral cowardice. But who is to say how we would have reacted had we been placed in her position? In the end, Webb gave evidence at the trial, and her fears were well founded: she left the household soon after. Catherine Light must also have had concerns about her son and his green bicycle, but a deep, maternal love often turns both eyes blind to an only son's obvious flaws.

PC Alfred Hall was promoted to sergeant in 1922 and served 25 years with the police. His was an ordinary career, uncrowned by any of the highest officer ranks, but his extraordinary conduct immediately after Bella's death has ensured he is not forgotten. Aged 47, he retired from the police force to become a publican, running the Rutland Arms Inn, near Grantham in Lincolnshire, and no doubt he regaled some of his regulars with the story of the Green Bicycle Case. He died in 1966, his memoir unfinished and unpublished.

Sir Edward Marshall Hall continued at the Bar until his death in early 1927. His biographer noted that he was never merely a counsel, but "a detective, showman, rhapsodist, actor". He performed all of these roles at the trial of Ronald Light, the first being perhaps the most important. Yet his extraordinary talents and achievements were drawn from his more ordinary experiences: the disappointments and difficulties that had shaped his own life.

After possibly spending some years abroad, Ronald Light changed his name to Leonard Estelle and moved to Kent. When he was nearly 50, he married. After World War II he reverted to using his real name. He appears to have led an ordinary life until his death in May 1975, at the age of 89.

It was a life denied to Annie Bella Wright. In a single moment, the domineering hand had moved the turning wheel and she was lost in a "treacherous bay swept to and fro" by the cruel tides of fate. It would be romantic to believe Bella would have led anything but an ordinary life, but we all too easily forget how wonderful such a life might have been. Out of the enormous swirls of space dust that form a hundred-billion galaxies, it is only when matter takes human form that it becomes truly astonishing. Coincidentally, for every galaxy in space we have a neuron in our brains, giving us each a universe of thought and emotion. We are able to speak, sing, laugh, love and reason – incredible capabilities that only we may possess.

Whether it is a woman lying in a lonely lane or a million men left behind on foreign fields, only when the young are cut down do we truly appreciate that an ordinary life is a most extraordinary and precious thing.

COLD CASE JURY
presents...
MOVE TO MURDER

The year is 1931. A telephone message is left at a chess club, instructing one of its members, insurance agent William Wallace, to visit a Mr Qualtrough. But the address given by the mystery caller does not exist and Wallace is forced to return home. By the time he returns to his quiet terraced house in Wolverton Street, Liverpool, he discovers that his wife, Julia, has been bludgeoned to death...

Who made the fatal call?
The police thought it was Wallace, creating an alibi for himself that might have come from an Agatha Christie thriller. Others believe him innocent but disagree on the identity of the murderer.

The Cold Case Jury must study the details and decide what happened in one of the most celebrated cold cases of all time.

Also by Mirror Books

Death at Wolf's Nick
Diane Janes

In January 1931, on a lonely stretch of Northumberland moorland known as Wolf's Nick, flames rose up into the night sky. Evelyn Foster, a young taxi driver, lay near her burning car, engulfed in flames, praying for a passing vehicle.

With her last breath, she described her attacker: a mysterious man with a bowler hat who had asked her to drive him to the next village, then attacked her and left her to die. Local police attempted to track down Evelyn's killer – while others questioned the circumstances, Evelyn's character and if there was even a man at all...

Professional crime writer and lecturer Diane Janes gained unprecedented access to Evelyn's case files. Through her evocative description, gift for storytelling and detailed factual narrative, Diane takes the reader back to the scene of the crime, painting a vivid description of village life in the 1930s.

Central to this tragic tale, is a daughter, sister and friend who lost her life in an horrific way – and the name of her murderer, revealed for the first time...

Also by Mirror Books

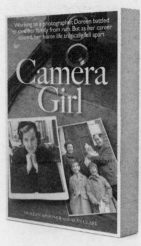

Camera Girl
Doreen Spooner with Alan Clark

The true story of a woman coping with a tragic end to the love of her life, alongside a daily fight to establish herself and support her children.

A moving and inspiring memoir of Doreen Spooner – a woman ahead of her time. Struggling to hold her head high through the disintegration of the family she loves through alcoholism, she began a career as Fleet Street's first female photographer.

While the passionate affair and family life she'd always dreamed of fell apart, Doreen walked into the frantic world of a national newspaper. Determined to save her family from crippling debt, her work captured the Swinging Sixties through political scandals, glamorous stars and cultural icons, while her homelife spiralled further out of control.

The two sides of this book take you through a touching and emotional love story, coupled with a hugely enjoyable portrait of post-war Britain.

Mirror Books

Also by Mirror Books
Published April 2017

The Boy in 7 Billion
Callie Blackwell and Karen Hockney

If you had a chance to save your dying son… wouldn't you take it?

Deryn Blackwell is a walking, talking miracle. At the age of 10, he was diagnosed with Leukaemia. Then 18 months later he developed another rare form of cancer called Langerhan's cell sarcoma. Only five other people in the world have it. He is the youngest of them all and the only person in the world known to be fighting it alongside another cancer, making him one in seven billion.
Told there was no hope of survival, after four years of intensive treatment, exhausted by the fight and with just days to live, Deryn planned his own funeral.

But on the point of death – his condition suddenly and dramatically changed. His medical team had deemed this an impossibility, his recovery was nothing short of a miracle. Inexplicable. However, Deryn's desperate mother, Callie, was hiding a secret…

Callie has finally found the strength and courage to reveal the truth about Deryn's battle. The result is a book that everyone should read.
It truly is a matter of life and death.

Also by Mirror Books

The Hunt for the 60s Ripper
Robin Jarossi

While 60s London was being hailed as the world's most fashionably vibrant capital, a darker, more terrifying reality was unfolding on the streets. During the early hours a serial killer was stalking prostitutes then dumping their naked bodies. When London was famed for its music, groundbreaking movies and Carnaby Street vibe, the reality included a huge street prostitution scene, a violent world that filled the magistrate's courts.

Seven, possibly eight, women fell victim – making this killer more prolific than Jack the Ripper, 77 years previously. His grim spree sparked the biggest police manhunt in history. But why did such a massive hunt fail? And why has such a traumatic case been largely forgotten today?

With shocking conclusions, one detective makes an astonishing new claim. Including secret police papers, crime reconstructions, links to figures from the vicious world of the Kray twins and the Profumo Affair, this case exposes the depraved underbelly of British society in the Swinging Sixties. An evocative and thought-provoking reinvestigation into perhaps the most shocking unsolved mass murder in modern British history.